TODAY'S WRITERS
AND THEIR WORKS

STEPHEN KING

TODAY'S WRITERS
AND THEIR WORKS

STEPHEN
KING

Rebecca Stefoff

 Marshall Cavendish
Benchmark
New York

With thanks to Tony Magistrale, Professor and Chair of the Department of English at the University of Vermont, for his expert review of this manuscript.

This publication represents the opinions and views of the author based on Rebecca Stefoff's personal experience, knowledge, and research. The information in this book serves as a general guide only. The author and publisher have used their best efforts in preparing this book and disclaim liability rising directly and indirectly from the use and application of this book.

Other Marshall Cavendish Offices:
Marshall Cavendish International (Asia) Private Limited, 1 New Industrial Road, Singapore 536196 • Marshall Cavendish International (Thailand) Co Ltd. 253 Asoke, 12th Flr, Sukhumvit 21 Road, Klongtoey Nua, Wattana, Bangkok 10110, Thailand • Marshall Cavendish (Malaysia) Sdn Bhd, Times Subang, Lot 46, Subang Hi-Tech Industrial Park, Batu Tiga, 40000 Shah Alam, Selangor Darul Ehsan, Malaysia

Marshall Cavendish is a trademark of Times Publishing Limited

All websites were available and accurate when this book was sent to press.

Library of Congress Cataloging-in-Publication Data
Stefoff, Rebecca, [date]-• Stephen King / by Rebecca Stefoff. • p. cm. — (Today's writers and their works) • Includes bibliographical references and index.
ISBN 978-0-7614-4122-9
1. King, Stephen, 1947—Juvenile literature. 2. Novelists, American—20th century— Biography—Juvenile literature. 3. Horror tales—Authorship—Juvenile literature. I. Title.
PS3561.I483Z877 2011 • 813'.54—dc22 • [B] • 2009033034

Publisher: Michelle Bisson. • Art Director: Anahid Hamparian
Series Designer: Alicia Mikles. • Photo research by Lindsay Aveilhe

The photographs in this book are used by permission and through the courtesy of: Weinstein Company/Everett Collection: cover; Susan Aimee Weinik/Time & Life Pictures/ Getty Images: 6; The Lurking Fear and Other Stories. H.P. Lovecraft. New York, NY: Ballantine Books, 1971: 10; Raul Touzon/Getty Images: 15; Everett Collection: 18; Newscom: 23, 137; Getty Images: 26, 79, 119; University of Maine: 31; Photos 12/Alamy: 39; Time & Life Pictures/Getty Images: 48 (top and bottom); Warner Bros/The Kobal Collection: 50; Columbia/Everett Collection: 68; Michael C. York/AP Photo: 71; Michael Ochs Archives/ Getty Images: 84, 87; United Artists/Getty Images: 89; United Artists/The Kobal Collection: 93; Castle Rock/WB/The Kobal Collection: 96; Castle Rock/Newscom: 99; AFP/Getty Images: 103; Castle Rock/WB/Time, Inc./Courtesy Jim Nolt: 108; Distant Horizon/The Kobal Collection: 110; FilmMagic/Getty Images: 126; Fabian Cevallos/Sygma/Corbis: 131.

Printed in Malaysia (T)
135642

CONTENTS

With the help of spooky props, Stephen King spoofed the image
of a horror writer in a 1985 commercial for American Express.
The commercial was part of a series featuring famous people from
many professions.

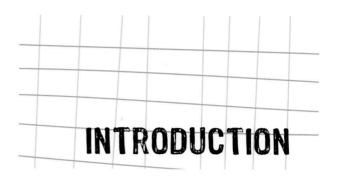

INTRODUCTION

WHY DO PEOPLE LIKE to be scared? What pleasure comes from reading tales of terror or from watching horror movies? One theory is that painful emotions, such as dread and revulsion, give some people a thrill—as long as they know that the source of their fear is "only a story," not something that can actually do harm. Another theory is that, when the story ends or the lights come on, the anxiety and discomfort produced by a scary book or film can lead to relief or even exhilaration.

In an essay titled "Why We Crave Horror Movies," Stephen King suggested that people watch horror films for the same reason they ride roller coasters: to prove to themselves or to others that they can do it. In addition, a horror movie can be a vacation for the conscious, rational, moral mind. A crazy, fearful, anti-civilized part of each of us, King claimed, usually stays deeply buried, but a horror movie lets that hidden self out for a little while to blow off steam.

Although King's essay was about movies, many who read it when it was published in 1981 must have felt that he was talking about horror fiction as well. After all,

Stephen King was then the best-known writer of horror in the world. King, who battled demons in his private life while depicting nightmares on the page, has become a phenomenon in American publishing, with more number-one best-selling books than any other author. His works have sold millions of copies in many countries, won him a vast legion of devoted fans, and launched scores of movies, television shows, and comics. Although "Stephen King" became a brand name and virtually a household word, the man himself has remained one of the hardest-working modern American writers, one who has experimented with new forms of storytelling during a career that spanned the final quarter of the twentieth century and continues into the twenty-first.

King has also been the subject of controversy. Because of their violent, graphic, or terrifying subject matter, some of his books have been banned from schools. The author himself withdrew one disturbing book from print. Critics have disagreed about King's talents as a writer and about the literary value of his books; the debate grew especially heated in 2003, when King won a major literary award. The works of King and of other writers whose output is sometimes called "genre fiction"—categories such as horror, mystery, fantasy, science fiction, and thriller—raise questions that critics cannot always easily answer: What are the differences between "serious" literature and "mere" entertainment? Who decides whether a book is one or the other?

Genre books are usually identified as popular, or pop, fiction, meaning that they are written to appeal to a wide audience. In this sense King is both an author of popular fiction and an extremely popular or successful author. Although his work has been studied in universities and published in literary magazines, his goal has always been to tell stories that anyone can read—and will want to keep reading. Using simple, everyday language, King creates recognizable settings, such as small towns and suburbs, and peoples them with characters who, for the most part, seem drawn from ordinary life, even though they find themselves in extraordinary, often desperate circumstances. Whether spinning versions of the vampire tale and the ghost story, weaving ambitious epics about decisive battles between good and evil, or exploring the passions of love and obsession in psychological thrillers, King does more than describe monsters "out there." He reveals the monsters inside human beings—and reveals the heroes, too.

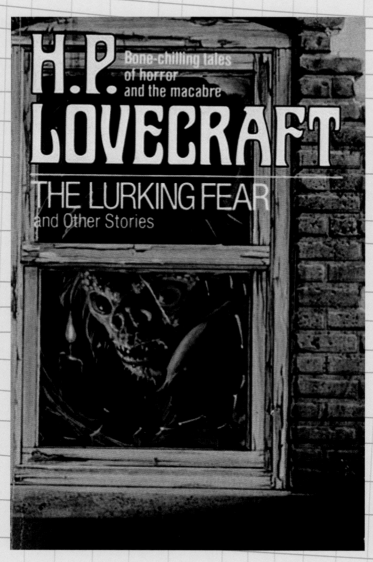

Young Stephen King discovered a paperback treasure in this collection of horror stories by H. P. Lovecraft. Although the book King read as a boy had a different cover, these tales helped set the course of King's own writing career.

THE BOX IN THE ATTIC

IT IS A SCENE STRAIGHT from a horror movie or a tale of fantastic adventure. A young hero wanders into a dangerous, deserted place, a silent chamber of old bones and forgotten secrets. The boy gazes for a long moment at a closed box, and then, as if he cannot stop himself, he slowly reaches out to open it . . .

In real life this scene unfolded on a chilly day in the autumn of 1959 or 1960. The setting was an attic in the town of Durham, Maine. The boy was around twelve years old, and his name was Steve King. What he found inside that box helped him become one of the best-known writers of all time.

The attic belonged to Steve's aunt and uncle, Ethelyn and Oren Flaws. Located above their garage, the attic was connected to the lofts over their barn. One loft contained the remains of chickens that had died long ago. Young Steve climbed up there sometimes to stare at them, fascinated by death and its mysteries. Years later he remembered the "chicken skeletons lying in a drift of feathers as ephemeral as moondust, some secret in the black sockets where their eyes had once been."

Steve and his older brother, Dave, were fascinated by the attic. It was a long, narrow room crowded with photographs, souvenirs, and stored items from their mother's family. Passageways barely wide enough for the boys snaked through piles of furniture and boxes. Walking was risky. The attic floorboards had never been nailed in place, and there were gaps between them. One misstep could have sent Dave or Steve plunging down to the garage floor. For this reason, although the brothers were not forbidden to go into the attic, their aunt and uncle disapproved of their explorations. Yet the boys were drawn to the place again and again. Some of those old boxes, they had discovered, held clues about the biggest mystery of their young lives: their missing father.

A year or so before the day when Steve opened the fateful box, the brothers had found an old reel of movie film in the attic. The film had been shot years earlier by Donald King, their father, who went to sea in the merchant marine service in the mid–1940s, during World War II. The boys had pooled their scanty money to get hold of a film projector so that they could watch the grainy footage, in which Donald King himself appeared briefly. Again and again the boys ran the film through their rented projector, anticipating the moment when their father looked into the camera, smiling and waving.

The brothers had also found some of their father's merchant marine mementos and scrapbooks commemorating his travels. For Steve, though, the most important relics of his father came to light later, on that autumn day when he opened a box he had not yet examined. In it he found what he later called "a treasure trove" of his father's books. They were paperbacks from the 1940s, books with garish covers and sometimes equally garish titles (one was *Burn, Witch, Burn*). One of the books was a collection of stories from *Weird Tales*, a magazine that published fantasy and horror fiction. The book that had the greatest impact on young Steve featured a fanged, red-eyed creature emerging from a tunnel beneath a tombstone. It was *The Lurking Fear and Other Stories*, a collection of works by the American pulp writer H. P. Lovecraft, which had been published in 1947, the year Steve was born.

King's later growth as a writer was shaped, in part, by his passionate embrace of a particular type of story, the kind of tale he loved to read and wanted to write. That box of books in the Flaws's attic showed him the way. The books were also one of his few connections to the father he never knew. They were the best legacy that Steve received from his absent parent.

Daddy Done

King's readers would one day grow familiar with the Maine settings of many of his stories and novels. The state's landscapes and townscapes and Mainers' habits and ways of speaking are woven into King's life and work. He did much of his growing up in Maine, the home of his mother's family.

Stephen King's mother, Nellie Ruth Pillsbury (called Ruth), was born in 1913. Her family, the Pillsburys, had lived in and around Scarborough, Maine, since 1790. She married young, in 1931, but that union soon ended in divorce. In

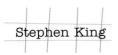

1939 Ruth married Donald Edwin King. Donald was born in 1914 in Peru, Indiana. He had family members living in Chicago, and the newly married couple lived there for a time before they relocated to New York State.

For most of World War II, Donald King was away for long stretches of time on his voyages. As the end of the war approached, however, he left the sea, and the couple returned to Maine. King took a job selling vacuum cleaners door-to-door in Scarborough. Believing that Ruth was unable to have children, in September 1945 the couple adopted a baby boy, whom they named David Victor. Ruth later became pregnant, and on September 21, 1947, she gave birth to a son, Stephen Edwin.

The marriage of Donald and Ruth was not a happy one. Stephen King described his father as "a man with an itchy foot, a travelin' man, as the song says." King added, "I think trouble came easy to him." His mother's comments were the only clues Steve could follow in his attempts to understand his father, because just after Steve's second birthday, Donald King told his wife one evening that he was going out to buy a pack of cigarettes. He left the house and never returned, and Steve grew up with no memory of his father.

Fortunately for the King boys, they had a strong mother who worked tirelessly not just to take care of them but also to fill them with confidence that they could deal with anything life dealt out to them. For years after her husband abandoned his family, Ruth and her sons moved from city to city, living first with one relative, then with another. They lived with King relatives in Illinois and Indiana and with Pillsbury relatives in Wisconsin and Connecticut. For a time

14

they rented an apartment near one of Ruth's sisters in Stratford, Connecticut, where Steve went to elementary school.

When Steve was eleven, Ruth and her sons moved back to Maine. They settled in with Ruth's parents in Durham, in a little neighborhood that King later described as "four families and a graveyard." The arrangement gave Ruth and the boys a home and provided a live-in caretaker for Ruth's parents. It also placed the boys near their aunt and uncle, in whose attic their mother had stored the relics of her vanished husband.

Throughout Dave's and Steve's childhood, their father was like "an unperson," King later recalled. Donald was

Stephen King grew up with no memory of the man who had deserted the family when he was two, but the house they moved into in Durham, Maine, had an attic packed full of his memorabilia.

rarely mentioned. Within the family he came to be called Daddy Done, which was short for "Daddy done left." Ruth told her sons that if anyone asked about their father, they should simply say that he was in the navy. "We were ashamed not to have a father," King said. "I think my mother was deeply ashamed to have been left with these two young boys when her other sisters kept their husbands."

Being without a father was never easy, but some moments were harder than others. When Steve was nine years old, he was alone in the Kings' Stratford apartment one October day watching a World Series game on television while his mother and brother were out. It was the day Don Larsen of the New York Yankees pitched a perfect game. The end of the game brought a pang of sadness as Steve thought of other boys watching and celebrating the game with their dads. The mem-ory of that sadness stayed with him for years.

The absent father, a central fact of King's childhood, later became a thread woven through his work. Michael Collings, who is both a literary critic and an acquaintance of King, has said, "The issue of his father's abandonment is in every-thing [he has written]. . . . Very rarely is there a functioning father in his stories." Some of King's fictional father-child relationships involve young people searching for fathers or father figures. Others concern men struggling—sometimes failing—to protect their children.

Fear and Fiction

One thing King did have during his childhood was a vivid imagination, often fed by strange or frightening stories, for which he had an endless appetite. As a very young child, he listened entranced to a radio broadcast of Ray Bradbury's eerie science fiction story "Mars Is Heaven" and then spent the night wide awake with a light on. Later, when King's mother read him *Strange Case of Dr. Jekyll and Mr. Hyde*, Robert Louis Stevenson's classic tale of a gentle doctor and his evil, murderous alter ego, he was struck by such details as Hyde crushing a little girl's bones—and he was filled with the desire to tell stories of his own that would be even more powerful.

The King boys loved comics. During the first grade, when Steve suffered a painful series of ear and throat infections that caused him to miss so much school that he had to repeat the grade, he read "approximately six tons of comic books," as he recalled in his book *On Writing*. Later he became especially fond of the gruesome stories and images found in *Tales from the Crypt*, *Castle of Frankenstein*, and similar publications. At one point Ruth got rid of Steve's stash of creepy comics because they gave him nightmares, but he craved the thrill and soon got his hands on more of them.

The boys also loved going to the movies as often as they could manage. Steve was especially fond of low-budget sci-fi and horror films such as *Earth vs. the Flying Saucers* (1956) and *I Was a Teenage Frankenstein* (1957). As King later explained, "I *liked* to be scared, I liked the total surrender of emotional control." Indeed, Steve was scared of a lot of things. His personal phobias included fear of spiders and of going insane. Other fears grew out of the climate of the times and were shared with millions of people. Shortly before King was born, World War II had ushered in the nuclear age, and the atomic bombs that the United States

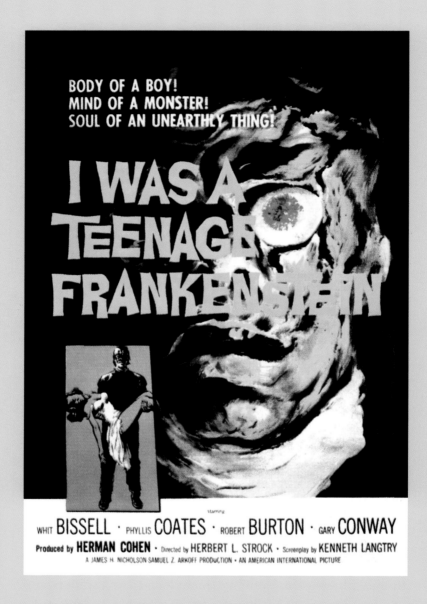

The King boys reveled in all things gruesome and scary. As often as they could afford it, they went to horror movies such as *I Was a Teenage Frankenstein* (1957), the story of a mad doctor who brings a dead high-school athlete back to life.

dropped on the Japanese cities of Hiroshima and Nagasaki had shown the world the terrifying destructive power of these new weapons. The 1950s and 1960s brought the cold war, in which the United States and the Soviet Union, a no-longer-existing communist state that then consisted of Russia and a number of neighboring countries, were locked in mutual suspicion and hostility. Many Americans feared that a global nuclear war between the two superpowers would destroy civilization. Those fears were reflected in the sci-fi and horror movies of King's childhood; in many of these films Earth or its inhabitants came close to being wiped out by aliens, plagues, or giant mutant monsters.

From an early age King was a writer as well as a reader. As a young child he copied the dialogue from *Combat Casey* comics onto a tablet of paper and added his descriptions of his own phrases. When he showed one of these efforts to his mother, she was delighted—until she realized that he had merely copied something. She handed the tablet back to him and said, "Write one of your own, Stevie. I bet you could do better."

King recalled in *On Writing* that those words had filled him with "an immense sense of *possibility*, as if I had been ushered into a vast building filled with closed doors and given leave to open any I liked. There were more doors than one person could ever open in a lifetime, I thought (and still think)." Responding to his mother's encouragement, King wrote a series of stories about Mr. Rabbit Trick, who drove around in a car with other friendly magic animals and helped kids. His mother rewarded him with a quarter for each of these stories. Other early King tales told of a town invaded by dinosaurs and a shoemaker hired by a king to kill witches.

King found a new outlet for his writing in 1959, when his brother began publishing an amateur newspaper called *Dave's Rag*. Dave wrote articles about local gossip and news. Steve wrote reviews of books and movies, as well as some stories. The brothers peddled the paper to neighbors, friends, and family. Soon King, barely into his teens, was also trying to get his work accepted in other markets. Banging away on an old typewriter in his attic bedroom, he wrote stories that he mailed off to such magazines as *Spaceman* and *Alfred Hitchcock's Mystery Magazine*. Not one story was accepted, but Steve built up a sizable collection of rejection slips (the notices that publishers send to authors whose work they have decided not to publish). He impaled the rejection slips on a nail in his wall. By the time he was fourteen, he needed a bigger nail.

By this time King had also discovered that box of his father's old paperbacks in his aunt and uncle's attic. Those books were a revelation. For one thing, they showed him that he and his father liked the same kinds of stories. (Ruth told her son that Donald had also written stories and tried to get them published but had given up when he failed to sell any.) Even more important was what the boy learned from reading those books. Unlike the B movies and comic books he devoured eagerly, the paperbacks were his "first encounter with serious fantasy-horror fiction," he later recalled in *Danse Macabre*, a survey of the horror genre. H. P. Lovecraft's stories made an especially strong impression because the young reader could tell that the writer "took his work seriously." King explains, "When Lovecraft wrote

'The Rats in the Walls' and 'Pickman's Model,' he wasn't simply kidding around or trying to pick up a few extra bucks; he *meant* it."

King took the books out of the attic and spent a week lost in their pages. A week or two later the paperbacks disappeared, perhaps spirited away by his aunt, who thought them unsuitable reading for a child. "[N]ot that it mattered in the long run," King said. "I was on my way. Lovecraft—courtesy of my father—had opened the way." Later King explored Lovecraft's stories in full, as well as the works of other writers inspired and influenced by Lovecraft, including Robert Bloch, best known as the author of *Psycho*, and Ray Bradbury. Lovecraft's shadow, King feels, lies over his own work and most of the important horror fiction created since the 1940s.

The Life of a Teenage Writer

Poverty was a constant presence in King's early life. The old Pillsbury house in Durham lacked a tub or shower, so the Kings had to shower at the Flaws's house, half a mile away. Ruth worked long hours taking care of her elderly parents in return for groceries given to her by other family members. The Kings ate a lot of lobster stew; far from being a delicacy, lobster was the cheap food of the poor in rural Maine in the 1950s and 1960s. The family had very little cash until King's grandparents died and his mother could go back to work. Even then money was scarce; the jobs she found—such as working in a home for the mentally disabled—paid very low wages. During President Lyndon B. Johnson's so-called War on Poverty in the mid–1960s,

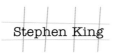

Ruth commented, "That's the war I'm in." Ruth had not learned to drive, so for some years the Kings were dependent on relatives and others for transportation.

When the King family settled in Durham, Steve attended fifth grade in one of the town's several one-room schoolhouses. By the time he reached the seventh grade, the town had built a larger school, where King mingled with a bigger population of classmates. One who became a friend recalled his first meeting with the tall, bespectacled King:

> He was the biggest kid in the class. I remember seeing him walking down the aisle between the desks, and I asked him how old he was, since he looked so much bigger than the rest of us. He looked down at me and said, "I'm old enough to know better, but I'm too young to care."

The same friend also remembered visiting King's small attic bedroom and finding it crammed with paperback books, mostly science fiction and horror. A typical teenager in many ways, King, like his friends, was interested in cars and popular music, but he also remained devoted to moviegoing, reading, and writing. During the seventh grade he wrote an eight-page story version of the 1961 film *The Pit and the Pendulum*, one of King's favorites among the movies he called Poepictures, films that were based (often very loosely) on the stories of the nineteenth-century American writer Edgar Allan Poe. King printed about forty copies of this production, took them to school in his bookbag, and sold every one for a quarter each. However, the principal made

The young Stephen King was strongly influenced by the work of Edgar Allan Poe. In seventh grade he wrote an eight-page story version of the movie version of Poe's classic tale of terror, *The Pit and the Pendulum*.

him return the money; he was told that school was not the place for him to peddle "junk like this." Junk or not, King continued to promote his own work (although not at school). During the summer following eighth grade, he sold roughly forty copies of an original tale called "The Invasion of the Star-Creatures." The next year he and a friend published a collection of eighteen one-page stories. King's contributions bore such titles as "The Dimension Warp," "The Thing at the Bottom of the Well," and "I've Got to Get Away!"

King went to high school in Lisbon Falls, a town not far from Durham. In his sophomore year he was made editor of the school paper, a job he found dull. Instead of putting out regular issues of the paper, he created an unofficial school publication he called *The Village Vomit*, which made fun of teachers. The students thought it was hilarious. The teachers, not so much. King almost got suspended, but in the end the most offended teacher settled for two weeks of detention and an apology. School officials decided that King had too much time on his hands and needed a more acceptable outlet for his desire to write. They arranged for him to get a job as sports writer for the local weekly paper, at half a cent a word. Although King didn't know much about sports, he liked getting paid for writing. However, the job's real value to him lay in what he learned from the paper's editor, John Gould, about the craft of writing.

In 1965 King finally received something he had awaited for years: an acceptance letter for one of his stories. The editor of a fanzine—an amateur magazine—called *Comics Review* published King's story "I Was a Teenage Grave-robber," although the title was changed to "In a Half-World of Terror." King was paid in copies of the magazine rather than in cash, but he regarded the "sale" as a milestone. He also had two stories published in the school paper during his senior year, and he wrote a play for Senior Night that, to the dismay of some of the teachers, was a satire of school personalities along the lines of *The Village Vomit*.

By the time King graduated from high school in 1966, he had college plans. Although he had been offered a partial scholarship to Drew University, in New Jersey, his mother could not afford to send him there; so instead, he attended the University of Maine at Orono, which was north of Durham near the city of Bangor. (His brother had graduated with honors from the same university in 1966.) King spent the summer between high school and college working at a cloth mill. "It wasn't the best summer I ever spent," he said later, "but I managed to avoid being sucked into the machinery or stitching my fingers together. . . ." That summer he heard wild stories about enormous rats said to inhabit the mill's basement. A few years later King put those tales to good use. First, however, came college, the social and political upheavals of the late 1960s, and the next stage of his evolution as a writer.

Stephen King would become almost as revolutionary in his later career at shaking the firmaments of the literary establishment as the civil rights marchers were in the 1960s.

MADE TO WRITE STORIES

"I WAS MADE TO WRITE STORIES and I love to write stories," Stephen King said. "That's why I do it. I really can't imagine doing anything else and I can't imagine not doing what I do." King wrote stories throughout his college years. After graduation, he struggled with unsatisfying jobs, money problems, and the challenge of starting a family but still continued to write. Making a living from writing was beginning to seem impossible—until three sheets of paper salvaged from a wastepaper basket turned things around and started King's rise to fame and fortune. He soon achieved the goal he had dreamed of for years: the life of a full-time writer.

The Spirit of the Times

King majored in English at Orono and also took courses in the College of Education at Orono, thinking that if he failed to make it as a writer he could be a teacher. By the time he graduated with a teaching certificate in 1970, King had, like many young people of the time, been caught up and transformed by the social movements and unrest that swept across America during those years.

The civil rights movement was changing race relations in the United States. In 1963, while King was in high school and nine years after the Supreme Court made racial segregation illegal in the nation's schools, Martin Luther King Jr. delivered his "I Have a Dream" speech in Washington, DC; Medgar Evers, of the National Association for the Advancement of Colored People, was murdered in Mississippi; and riots broke out in Birmingham, Alabama, after four girls died in a bomb explosion at a church that had hosted civil rights meetings. King's college years saw race riots in several major American cities and, in 1968, the assassination of Martin Luther King Jr. Despite tragedies and losses, however, the civil rights movement succeeded in changing laws and policies involving race. It was one aspect of a societal upheaval that some Americans found intoxicating and others found threatening. Another source of discord was feminism and the women's movement, whose aim was redefining the role of women in society. A number of laws passed in the 1960s sought to end discrimination against women in the workplace. In addition, the National Organization for Women was formed in 1966, and topics such as domestic abuse and sexual harassment began to be discussed openly.

Vietnam was perhaps the most turbulent and divisive element in the America of the late 1960s. A war had been raging between communist and anticommunist forces in Southeast Asia for years by the time the United States sent military advisers to anticommunist South Vietnam in the early 1960s. By 1965 U.S. combat troops were fighting in the jungles of Vietnam. As the Johnson administration increased American involvement in the war throughout the mid–1960s, an antiwar movement formed in protest. Students across the nation took a leading part. They marched in demonstrations and, on many campuses, organized sit-ins (occupation of school buildings) to protest the "business as usual" attitude of mainstream institutions toward the war.

Although the Vietnam War continued until the mid–1970s, the protest movement and the spirit of change had a profound effect on King during his college years. When he arrived in Orono to start college, he was in many ways a conservative. He had been raised in his mother's Methodist religion and had absorbed the Republican politics of his family and community. Growing outrage over the Vietnam War, along with exposure to new ideas, drew him toward more liberal views.

In August 1968, King was one of thousands of students who made their way to Chicago during the Democratic Party's national convention. Their purpose was to take part in antiwar protests and show support for Senator Eugene McCarthy, who was competing with Lyndon Johnson for the party's presidential nomination. When protestors and police clashed, King was temporarily blinded by a shot of police mace but managed to escape the scene without serious injury. His opposition to the Vietnam War continued; a photograph in the school's 1969 yearbook shows a bearded King, the student body president, urging his fellow students to join him in protesting the war. By the time he graduated from college in 1970, King had shifted his political allegiance to the Democrats, and since then he has publicly supported Democratic political candidates.

Along with antiwar activism, recreational drug use was widespread in the youth counterculture of the times. King and his friends took part in that activity, as well. King, in later discussions about his use of LSD and other hallucinogens, said that he did not recommend them. He was also drinking regularly by his college years; this habit, in time, became an addiction and then a crisis.

On college campuses across the land, the late 1960s brought a widespread questioning of authority, a demand for new ways of doing things. For King that spirit applied to the teaching of literature. As in most universities, the English Department of the University of Maine at Orono offered courses based in what is sometimes called the canon: the body of works—including the ancient Greek dramas, the plays and poetry of Shakespeare, and the works of the modern writers Henry James and James Joyce, among many others— that critics and cultural historians have long identified as representing the best of Western literature. In the late 1960s, however, some students and academics began criticizing the narrowness of the canon, which they derided as the work of "dead white males." Within a decade universities responded by adding courses in material outside the traditional canon: works by women and nonwhites, works from cultures other than those of western Europe and the United States, and more works by living writers.

King wanted his university to move beyond the canon in a different way. He said that the school should offer a course

Like many people of his generation, Stephen King was transformed by the social upheavals and political turmoil of the late 1960s.

in popular fiction: mystery, fantasy, and similar genres—the kinds of books King had been reading voraciously for years. He even offered to teach such a course. Although King was probably better versed in the subject than anyone on the faculty, the university was not ready to let an undergraduate teach. Demand for the course was sufficiently great, however, that the university added it to the spring 1969 schedule. The official instructor was a member of the English Department, but in reality the course was created and taught by his assistant, Stephen King. It was the first course in popular fiction ever taught at the University of Maine at Orono, and it reflected King's unswerving belief that popular fiction was not all "junk," as his high school principal had termed it. Popular fiction could be and often was good fiction that deserved to be taken seriously. The course was a victory for King, but this would not be his last clash with the canon.

All through college, King kept writing. By this time he was getting published—and not just in *Ubris*, the school's literary magazine, where a number of his stories and a few poems appeared, or in the college paper, where he wrote a weekly column. In 1967 he made his first professional cash sale when *Startling Mystery Stories* paid him thirty-five dollars for a story called "The Glass Floor." By the time he graduated from college, King had sold a few more stories and accumulated a stack of unpublished manuscripts, including several novels. After graduating from college, he wrote a story that began with the line, "The man in black fled across the desert and the gunslinger followed." The college paper published the story in eight parts under the title "Slade." Later that seed grew into one of King's most complex works.

The Turning Point

During the summer of 1969, while working in the university library, King had met a fellow student worker named Tabitha Spruce. That fall, as the two got to know one another in a poetry seminar, they fell in love. Before long Spruce and King were living together. When Spruce became pregnant, she was a junior and King was finishing his senior year, which included working as a student teacher. Their daughter, Naomi Rachel King, was born soon after King's graduation. King and Spruce married in January 1971.

Although King emerged from college with a teaching certificate, he had to stay in Orono for Tabitha's senior year, and jobs were scarce. He took what work he could get, first pumping gas, then pressing sheets in a laundry in Bangor. The need to write had not deserted him, and he kept submitting stories to magazines. "Graveyard Shift," a story based on the rumors he had heard about huge rats in the basement of the cloth mill where he used to work, sold to *Cavalier* magazine in 1970. Over the next few years the magazine published more of King's stories, but although the two or three hundred dollars King received for each story was a welcome addition to the family income, the Kings were barely scraping by. The best job Tabitha could get after graduating was in a doughnut shop. King landed a position teaching English at Hampden Academy, the school where he had been a student teacher; during summers he returned to work at the laundry. After the Kings' second child, Joseph Hillstrom, was born in 1972, the family moved to a trailer. King set up a chair, table, and typewriter in the trailer's small laundry room. When the family later moved to a small apartment, King carved out a writing space there as well. He spent several hours there almost every night banging out stories.

King was also trying to sell his novels. An editor at Doubleday named William Thompson liked several of them but could not persuade the company to take a chance on King. Tabitha, a strong supporter of her husband as well as an astute critic of his work, told him not to take a part-time job that would have cut into his writing time, even though the family needed money. She praised her husband's work when she liked it—and gave him suggestions on how to improve it when she did not. King has called her "my ideal reader."

One day in 1972, King came home from his teaching job to find Tabitha waiting for him with three wrinkled sheets of paper. She had seen them crumpled up in the wastebasket in King's writing room and smoothed them out to read them. They were the opening pages of a story King had started, about a girl who is terrified when her first menstrual period starts at school and then humiliated when the other girls mock her. King had thrown the pages away because it did not feel natural to him to tell a story from a female point of view; he also feared that the story would be too long for the magazines that were buying his work.

Tabitha thought otherwise. "You've got something here," she told her husband. "I really think you do." She told him to finish telling the story, no matter how many pages it took, and she answered his questions about high school girls' locker rooms and social behavior. By December 1972 the story had become a short novel that ends in violence and destruction when the girl strikes back at her tormentors with mental powers she gained when she began menstruating. King called the book *Carrie*. He sent the manuscript to Thompson at Doubleday, who thought that King had a real chance of selling this one to the publishing company, and then King went back to his routine of teaching and writing stories.

A few months later Doubleday offered an advance of

$2,500 to publish King's novel. It was not a lot of money for a first novel, even in the 1970s, but it meant that King would be a professional novelist at last, with a better chance of selling other novels. He and Tabitha stayed up all night, giddy with excitement, talking about the possibilities. When the money arrived, they used it to buy a new car. King signed on for another year of teaching at Hampden Academy. Then he received a call from Thompson, informing him that Doubleday had just sold the rights to publish a paperback edition of *Carrie* for $400,000. Under the terms of his Doubleday contract, the publisher received half of the money, King the other half. In addition, the company wanted to see another manuscript.

That call changed everything. King was bursting to share the news with Tabitha, but she was not home. In a daze, he went across the street to the drugstore and bought her a gift, the only thing he could find—a hair dryer.

The Long Road to Overnight Success

King's professional life moved fast after *Carrie* appeared in bookstores in April 1974. That month a Maine newspaper reported, "*Carrie* is expected to be a household word around Durham and Lisbon Falls soon with the recent publication of Steve King's book"; people in the area were eager for *Carrie* to appear in local bookstores because they wanted to read a novel by "a local boy everybody knew." King, it was predicted, would "put Durham on the map."

Carrie was not a big seller in hardcover, but the paperback—which appeared in April 1975—was a success, selling more than a million copies in less than a year. King also

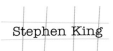

sold the movie rights to the book. By the end of 1974, in addition to placing a few stories in magazines, King had sold the hardcover and paperback rights to another novel, a vampire tale called *'Salem's Lot*; his share of the paperback rights earned him a quarter of a million dollars.

Like *Carrie*, *'Salem's Lot* was set in a world King knew very well: the Maine of rural towns and small cities, tied together by lonely roads running through the forest. King had long admired the power of the first widely successful vampire novel, Bram Stoker's *Dracula*, published in 1897. Once, when King speculated over dinner that a serious vampire story set in modern America would not work because mass media and crime-fighting technology would make it difficult for a vampire to escape notice, Tabitha and a friend remarked that anyone could hide away from the world in the small towns of rural Maine. Thinking about those remarks, King reflected that places like those in which he had grown up were ideal settings for horror fiction:

> There are so many small towns in Maine,
> towns which remain so isolated that almost
> anything could happen there. People could
> drop out of sight, disappear, perhaps even
> come back as the living dead.

While in college King had written a story set in a fictional nineteenth-century Maine community called Jerusalem's Lot. He returned to that setting, updated and shortened to 'Salem's Lot, for the vampire novel he wrote in tribute to Stoker. It was an inspired decision. The critic Leonard Wolf noted in a discussion of *'Salem's Lot* that "one of the things King does best is rendering the feel of American small-town life." By embedding his story of monstrous horror in a setting he could describe accurately and in detail, King gave the story a quality of realism.

Although King is famous primarily as a writer of horror and suspense, he is also a regional writer—one whose work reflects and embodies not just the geography of a certain region but its attitudes and ways of life as well. According to Tony Magistrale of the University of Vermont, "King's Maine is a place of terrifying loneliness where nature seems antagonistic to human habitation and where men and women often feel the same degree of estrangement from one another as they do toward the supernatural creatures who threaten their lives. . . . His north country is a region of a particular people, language, and customs, all set apart by an awareness of their difference from cities even as near as Boston."

By the time he sold *'Salem's Lot*, King was working on the manuscript that would become his third published novel. For this book, *The Shining*, King shifted to a different setting—the Rocky Mountains of the American West. King decided to use a Colorado setting because he and his family were living there at the time. His mother had died of cancer in December 1973, and after her death and the other changes in his life, King, now a full-time writer, wanted a change of scene from the state where he had lived since the age of eleven. So he and Tabitha and their children drove to the Rocky Mountains in a new Cadillac and temporarily relocated to a rented house in Colorado.

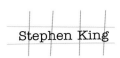

'Salem's Lot hit the bookstores on the day before Halloween in 1975. Like *Carrie*, it failed to make much of a splash in hardcover but sold very well later in paperback. This success raised expectations for King's next novel.

In *'Salem's Lot*, King had taken on the vampire. In *The Shining* he tackled another element of classic horror and supernatural fiction, the haunted house. More accurately, it is a haunted hotel—the huge, brooding Overlook, perched high in the mountains, isolated for months each winter, and filled with the angry, anguished ghosts of those who had suffered and died there in the past. Into this setting King sent a fragile family, including an abusive, alcoholic father named Jack Torrance and his son, Danny, who can sometimes read minds, communicate telepathically (through mental power alone), and foresee the future. The evil forces of the hotel—represented throughout the book by the symbol of a buzzing nest of dark, angry wasps—forge a link with Jack. They awaken a despair and violence that Jack is unable to suppress. The climax of the novel is a deadly confrontation between father and son. Jack Torrance perishes, consumed by the fiery explosion of the hotel; Danny finds a source of strength and guidance—a father figure—in Dick Hallorann, a black man who was formerly a caretaker at the hotel.

Reactions to *The Shining* were mixed. When William Thompson, King's first editor, read the manuscript, he thought it was the best thing King had written. Others agreed, and more recently, one King scholar has called *The Shining* "an inventive, rich novel that brought together many of King's strengths." A reviewer for the *New York Times*, however, had little good to say about the novel.

In a memorable scene from the 1980 film *The Shining*, Jack Torrance—played by actor Jack Nicholson—breaks into the bathroom where his terrified wife is hiding. More than a simple ghost story, *The Shining* explores themes of abuse, alcoholism, and insanity.

He criticized King's writing style; he found King's use of capital letters, italics, and exclamation points to highlight urgent thoughts and emotions, for example, gimmicky and distracting—although he did admit that the book had "its chilling moments." According to another review in the same paper, *The Shining* was "fairly engaging and preposterous claptrap." The reviewer stated that while the book showed King's energy as a writer, it was too overloaded with plot elements and horror clichés to explore the "core of psychological truth" in the relationship between Jack and his wife, Wendy. Whatever the *New York Times* reviewers thought, King's third novel was a hit with readers. When released in 1977, *The Shining* sold 50,000 copies and became the first Stephen King book to reach the *New York Times* bestseller list—the gold standard of success in publishing—in hardcover. The paperback sold more than 2 million copies.

Writers' careers usually contain a few false starts: story ideas that do not develop as expected, novels that never get finished, or work that remains unpublished. King is no exception. Before he wrote *The Shining*, he had started several novels, only to abandon them. By the time he entered the final stages of work on *The Shining*, however, he was deep into writing another novel, one that grew out of his short story "Night Surf," which had been published in his college literary magazine in 1968 and in *Cavalier* in 1974.

"Night Surf" describes a night in the lives of a handful of kids who think they have survived a worldwide influenza plague that they call Captain Trips.

That brief tale became the starting point for a long, ambitious novel that King titled *The Stand*, a story of the apocalypse—the destruction of civilization and much of the human race—and what happens afterward. *The Stand* describes the devastation that occurs when a man-made "superflu" virus, created as a biological weapon, escapes from a military facility and kills more than 99 percent of the world's population. In a final battle for the soul of what remains of humankind, the survivors align themselves with the forces of good and evil, represented by a saintly black woman called Mother Abagail and a demonic man named Randall Flagg, called the Dark Man or the Walkin' Dude.

The Stand was published in 1978, as was *Night Shift*, a collection of short stories that includes "Night Surf" and "Jerusalem's Lot," which King had written for a college class and which is full of references to King's early inspiration, H. P. Lovecraft. Next came the novel *The Dead Zone* (1979), about a man who recovers from a coma with the ability to see the future of anyone he touches. For this novel King returned to a New England setting: Maine and neighboring New Hampshire. The following year *Firestarter* was published. It is the story of a girl who, like Carrie, possesses an unusual and potentially destructive power—the result, this time, of a secret government experiment. Unlike Carrie, however, the young heroine of *Firestarter* has a father who loves her and sacrifices himself to save her life.

By that time King had ended his relationship with Doubleday. He had become frustrated with contract terms that he felt gave the company too much control over his earnings and too large a piece of the income from the sale of paperback rights. In addition, he was unhappy that Doubleday had forced him to cut the manuscript of *The Stand* by about a third. The company claimed that publishing the uncut manuscript, which was more than 1,200 pages long, would be far too expensive. With the help of a literary agent who had been selling his stories, King formed relationships with two other publishing companies. New American Library, a paperback publisher, bought the rights to publish new books and sold the hardcover rights to Viking. This was the first of several times that King changed publishers as his career evolved.

King's rapid rise to multiple-book best-sellerdom amazed some observers. In 1977, a writer for the *Bangor Daily News* marveled, "It's a long way from teaching English at Hampden Academy to selling 5 million copies of three books, all of which have been sold to the movies. But Stephen King, 29, has made that stupendous jump in only three years." By the time *Firestarter* was published three years later, King was a multimillionaire, a publishing phenomenon with six novels and a short-story collection to his credit. King may have looked like an overnight success, but in reality he had spent years mastering the craft of writing and struggling time and again to get published.

King's rise also owed something to changing fashions in American publishing and moviemaking. Horror and the supernatural had been out of fashion for many years until the late 1960s, when, as in so many aspects of American culture, tastes began to change. Two highly successful works led the way. Ira Levin's novel of satanic impregnation, *Rosemary's Baby*, was published in 1967 and made into an award-winning film the following year. William Peter Blatty's *The Exorcist*, a novel of demonic possession featuring a girl with strange and deadly powers, was published in 1971 and became a hit movie in 1973. By the time *Carrie* arrived the following year, Americans were eager for more supernatural thrills and chills. The horror genre, once a small and low-budget part of the publishing and film worlds, experienced a boom that lasted through the 1970s and into the 1980s. That boom saw the emergence of writers such as Anne Rice (whose series of vampire novels appeared beginning in 1976), Dean R. Koontz, Clive Barker, and Dan Simmons, as well as filmmakers such as Wes Craven and David Cronenberg. As an early arrival on the horror scene, King both helped create the boom and benefited from it. His success was due partly to his own talent and energy and partly to fortunate timing and the shrewd marketing of his early horror blockbusters.

Screen

The film version of *Carrie*, directed by Brian de Palma, was released in 1976 and became a box office success. Sissy Spacek starred as Carrie; the cast also included Piper Laurie and John Travolta. The movie earned Oscar nominations for Laurie and Spacek, and it boosted paperback sales of both *Carrie* and *'Salem's Lot*. King was happy about the way the movie turned out—such was not always the case with film adaptations of his work. As judged by King himself, as well as film critics and the viewing public, the many efforts to translate King's work to the screen have been a mixed bag: some were successes, some were howling duds, and a lot of productions fell somewhere in the middle. King's relationship with the visual media has been complex and has produced results as uneven as that of any popular writer.

The next King novel to be filmed was *'Salem's Lot*, which was made into a four-hour television miniseries because studio executives thought it would be too difficult to adapt such a complex story into a film script. Shot in California, the miniseries was directed by Tobe Hooper, who had directed the notorious slasher film *The Texas Chainsaw Massacre* (1974) and who later directed Steven Spielberg's *Poltergeist* (1982), a story of ghostly posssession. Again, King was pleased with the result, although he regretted the fact that the network television standards of the time forced some watering-down of crucial elements, such as violent vampire attacks on, and threats to, children.

King was less satisfied with the film version of *The Shining*, released in 1980. Directed by Stanley Kubrick—who had made *2001: A Space Odyssey* (1968) and *A Clockwork Orange* (1971)—the film stars Jack Nicholson in the role of Jack Torrance. The movie disappointed King, who felt that Kubrick did not understand how to use the raw materials of the horror genre for maximum impact. The author complained that "nothing in the movie is really scary. . . . It's like this great big gorgeous car with no engine in it— that's all." Many film critics admired Kubrick's subtle use of special effects and atmosphere, however, and audiences generally loved Nicholson's over-the-top performance as the disturbed and eventually deranged Jack Torrance.

Finding Home

During the late 1970s, King and his family were on the move. In 1975 the Kings left Colorado and returned to Maine. "We didn't feel comfortable in Colorado," King later said; he recalled that even while living in Colorado, he created characters who spoke and acted like working-class Mainers. The Kings bought a house in Bridgton, in the western part of Maine. Two years later, their third child, Owen Phillip, was born. By that time King was again restless and hungry for new surroundings; so in late 1977 he and Tabitha put the house on the market, packed up their things, and moved with their three children to a rented house in England.

King had decided to spend a year in what he called "the land of the ghost story." He found, however, that the move to England did not fire up his creative energies in the way that he had expected. Instead of the ghost story he had planned to write, he found himself writing the first draft of a novel called *Cujo*, about a rabid dog in the town of Castle Rock, a Maine community that King had invented in *The Dead Zone* and later used as the setting for many other works. King also formed a friendship with the American horror writer Peter Straub, who was living in London at the time; the two men later collaborated on several books. After three months, the Kings were ready to go home. Once more they returned to Maine, where King purchased a house for his family on a lake in Center Lovell.

Before long, King found himself back in Bangor, at the University of Maine in Orono. His alma mater invited him to return for the 1978–1979 academic year as a visiting writer to teach courses in creative writing, poetry, and literature to first-year students. At the urging of a former professor and mentor, King accepted the invitation. Other members of the English department during King's year were impressed that King did not act like a celebrity. He took on the full range of an instructor's duties, including sitting on committees and dealing with administrative matters. King enjoyed his temporary return to the classroom, even though, as he explained to an interviewer a few years later, he did not believe that creativity could be taught:

I think that you can teach writers who have come a certain distance to do things that make their writing better. You can teach things about point of view, for example. You can teach things about pace. But you cannot teach a writer to find the good story, the story that hasn't been told. With writers who are very good—the naturals—you can't really do anything except give them an environment of friendly criticism, and let them read the story to the class. Hopefully, the teacher's input and the class's input will mean something to the writer in terms of grasping or rewriting that story or the next story more firmly.

During King's first semester of teaching, he received an interesting suggestion from William Thompson, his former editor at Doubleday, now with another publishing company. Thompson invited King to write a nonfiction book—a history of horror in fiction, film, and popular culture. King agreed. In writing the book he drew upon material he had prepared for teaching a class in supernatural literature; he also tapped into his lifelong immersion in weird and supernatural fiction and worked autobiographical revelations into the book. King's survey of the roots, themes, and writers of modern horror fiction was published under the title *Danse Macabre* in 1981. It is still regarded as a valuable contribution to the study of the horror genre. Scholars who study King find in *Danse Macabre* a road map to his early interests and influences.

During King's teaching stint at the University of Maine, his family occupied a rented house on the outskirts of Bangor. A busy highway near the house was the source of two memorable incidents—a terrifying moment when young Owen darted toward the highway and the tragic death of Naomi's pet cat, which was hit by a truck and then buried in a place where the neighborhood kids interred animals killed on the road. Those events got King started on a new novel, *Pet Sematary*, the story of a man whose two-year-old is killed on a highway and then brought back to a disturbing, zombielike half-life by the mysterious powers of a secret burial ground. King was appalled to have had such a frightening vision of a child's death and dark resurrection, and both Tabitha and Peter Straub agreed that the book was too disturbing to be published. King tucked the manuscript away and moved on.

Among other projects, King returned to *The Gunslinger*, a novel he had written based on his tale "Slade," which had appeared in King's college newspaper in 1970. King's original inspiration for the story, like many of his ideas, was born out of the combination of two unrelated elements. In the case of *The Gunslinger*, the first element was the 1855 poem "Childe Roland to the Dark Tower Came" by the British poet Robert Browning, which tells of a heroic knight's doomed quest through a desolate land toward a mysterious tower. The other element was the spaghetti western films of the Italian director Sergio Leone—movies, such as *The Good, the Bad, and the Ugly* (1966), that portrayed tough, lonely, larger-than-life heroes and villains in an imaginative version of the Wild West. King had wondered what would

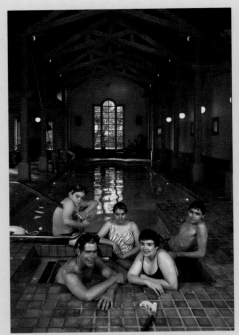

Stephen and Tabitha King's children (left to right, Owen, Naomi, and Joe) grew up in a mansion that King equipped with a new office, an indoor pool, and even a secret passage.

To discourage unwanted visitors, King surrounded the family's Bangor house with a fence decorated with bats and spiderwebs. Some of his journeys through its gates took place on two wheels. In 1994 he rode a Harley across the country to promote his novel *Insomnia*.

happen if he combined the two forms: the romantic, knightly quest and the gritty western. The result was *The Gunslinger*. Rather than being the kind of horror story to which King's fans were becoming accustomed, the novel was the beginning of an epic fantasy about the battle between good and evil across different planes of existence—his version of J. R. R. Tolkien's *The Lord of the Rings*, as he sometimes referred to it. King reworked his earlier draft and offered it to the *Magazine of Fantasy and Science Fiction*, which published it in five installments between 1978 and 1981.

After King's teaching job ended, the Kings decided to settle in Bangor. The unpretentious, working-class town appealed to King, who thought that it would be a good place for him to work. The perfect house was available, too: a twenty-four room mansion, built in the 1850s, on a seven-acre estate. As a teenager, Tabitha told King, she had stared at the place, fantasizing about living there someday. Once the Kings had bought the property, they spent three years remodeling it to suit their needs. Offices were created for King and his wife (Tabitha also wrote fiction, in addition to helping manage the business aspects of her husband's career). A swimming pool was built inside a barn, and a large modern kitchen was added. When uninvited visitors and curiosity seekers became a problem, King had the entire property surrounded by a wrought-iron fence ornamented with bats and spiders. After the family moved into their new home, King settled down in his office, which featured a hidden passage and a concealed doorway covered by a bookcase, to maintain the work schedule that had made him so prolific and successful.

An alien fungus conquers Stephen King in *Creepshow*. The writer, who had previously acted in a tiny role in the 1981 movie *Knightriders*, has appeared in many of the movies and miniseries based on his work.

3

KING CROWNED

"**THE BOTTOM LINE**," Stephen King told an interviewer in 1986, "is that a lot of the time now I'm too busy *being* Stephen King to write." By the 1980s, being Stephen King involved much more than writing books. It encompassed giving interviews about the books, touring to promote the books, writing screenplays for movies and television shows based on the books, and directing or acting in some of those movies. All the while, compelled by his need to write, King produced new books, some of which were published under a pseudonym.

In addition to being brought down by addiction in the 1980s and by a near-fatal accident when he was struck by a van in 1999, King also persevered through stretches of writer's block. In spite of these obstacles, his output remained prodigious. Although the label "horror writer" persisted, King explored other genres; he also experimented with alternative methods of reaching his readers, including serial novels and online publication. By the year 2000 King's white-hot fame had cooled somewhat and so had the pace of his work. Yet although he had spoken many times of retiring,

he continued to publish. Meanwhile critics debated whether King had run out of fresh ideas or was getting better as he got older.

The 1980s

Maximum Overdrive is the title of a 1986 movie written and directed by King, based on his story "Trucks," about rebellious vehicles with wills of their own. The phrase "maximum overdrive" could also be applied to King's life and his work output throughout much of the 1980s, a decade that saw the publication of fifteen novels and two collections of shorter work. Even though some of this work had been written before 1980, it added up to a lot of pages. He was also writing things that would not appear until after the decade ended. Besides books, he began writing screenplays; he also did some acting, directed a feature film, and launched new publishing ventures.

The 1980s: Books

The first of King's novels published in the 1980s was *Cujo* (1981), in which a rabid dog terrorizes a woman and her son. The novel, set in King's fictional town of Castle Rock, employed an unusual form—there are no chapter breaks, but simply a series of passages that narrate the story from various points of view. Next came *The Gunslinger*, which was published in 1982 in book form by a small publishing company that specialized in fantasy works.

King was not finished with the story of Roland Deschain, the gunslinger. He intended to continue Roland's quest— *The Gunslinger* was only the first installment of a larger work King called *The Dark Tower*—but he was not sure exactly how or when he would do so. For years after *The Gunslinger* appeared, King was besieged by questions and demands from fans. Partly in response to these questions, he launched a newsletter for fans in 1985. In the pre-Internet 1980s, the *Castle Rock* shared news of King with his readers and answered their questions publicly, as his official website (stephenking.com) does today. When *The Drawing of the Three*, the second volume of *The Dark Tower*, was ready for publication in 1987, King gave his loyal fans a gift by releasing the first chapter of the book in the *Castle Rock* a month before the book was issued by the same small specialty publisher. The following year, because of reader demand for greater availability of the *Dark Tower* books, *The Gunslinger* appeared in paperback form; *The Drawing of the Three* followed in 1989.

The newsletter was only one of King's new media. In 1982 he founded his own private publishing company, Philtrum Press, to issue limited editions of a few writings. Among its first publications were installments of a tale called *The Plant*. King had sent an installment of this work each year for three years to friends at Christmas. In 1982 King also collaborated on *Creepshow*, a graphic novel for which King wrote the text and Bernie Wrightson drew the illustrations. It consisted of five stories, two of which had been published before, and was the basis for a movie released in the same year.

The year 1983 saw the publication of three King books. *Christine* is the story of a cursed vintage car that is possessed by a vengeful demon. *Cycle of the Werewolf* is a collection of linked stories about werewolves; like the *Dark Tower* books, it was published first in hardcover by a small specialty press and later in paperback for the general market. The third book was *Pet Sematary*, the novel King had once thought too ghoulish even for his readers. Its publication settled a long-standing dispute with Doubleday, his former publisher, which agreed to pay King all the royalties the company still owed him in a single sum (rather than over a long period of time as the original contract specified) if he would give them a new book to publish. He gave them *Pet Sematary*. Not only was it a best seller, but it won praise from some critics.

The Talisman, a dark fantasy novel that King wrote with Peter Straub, was published in 1984; the two men had taken turns writing sections of the manuscript. The premise of *The Talisman*, like that of the *Dark Tower* books, is that the natural world coexists with another, parallel world. Although the two worlds occupy different dimensions, or planes of being, certain people and creatures can pass between them. The hero of *The Talisman*, a teenager named Jack Sawyer, goes from the natural world into the magical, perilous world, known as The Territories, in the hope of finding a cure for his mother's cancer.

A literary secret came to light at this point in King's career. The king of horror had published five novels that few people knew about and even fewer had read because they appeared under the name Richard Bachman. King had invented Bachman in 1977 in a confidential arrangement with New American Library, which became his paperback publisher at that time. Under this agreement, New American Library released some of King's earlier, unpublished novels that did not seem to fit into the "Stephen King" body of work because they were short, taut thrillers or suspense dramas rather than the long supernatural stories that readers associated with King's name. The agreement may have sprung from King's and his publisher's fear of overloading the marketplace with Stephen King books or of confusing readers; King was also genuinely curious about what reaction these early books would receive if readers did not know they were the work of the now-famous author.

In an essay titled "The Importance of Being Bachman," Stephen King explained the role of the Bachman pseudonym in his creative life. Many of King's books, despite their often terrifying and gruesome subject matter, end on an optimistic note—a triumph of love, courage, or at least survival. His work reflects a spirit of hope that basic human decency will prevail. In contrast, "the Bachman state of mind," was "low rage and simmering despair," as King described it. Bachman, King said, gave a voice to his darker side—"a good voice and a valid point of view that were a little different from my own."

The original Bachman books were *Rage* (1977), the story of a high school student who brings a gun to school and takes his classmates hostage; *The Long Walk* (1979), about teenage boys in a deadly contest in a near-future American dictatorship; *Roadwork* (1981), in which a grieving man suffers a violent breakdown when he learns that his house will be demolished to make room for a highway; and *The Running Man* (1982), another science fiction story of deadly competition in the near future. Initially, the Bachman books made little impression on readers and critics. By the time New American Library released Bachman's fifth novel,

Thinner, in 1984, rumors of the author's true identity were afoot. In the *Washington Post* review of *Thinner*, Everett F. Bleiler mentioned that many horror fans suspected that Bachman was King. He added that *Thinner* "is not good King, although here and there the power of the major King flashes out." King acknowledged his Bachman identity in early 1985. As a result, sales of *Thinner* jumped from 28,000 to almost 300,000 copies by the end of the year. The earlier Bachman books, reissued in a single volume, became a best seller, and King sold the movie rights to *The Running Man*. The critic S. T. Joshi, author of a number of studies of horror fiction, has argued that these Bachman books— "written with verve, flair, and a bracing toughness of setting, conception and mood"—are superior to the books King has published under his own name, which Joshi regards as sentimental and unoriginal. Some of the Bachman books have remained in print, but in the late 1990s, after reading reports that a Kentucky student who shot and killed other students had possessed a copy of *Rage*, King withdrew that book from the marketplace.

Between the revelation of Bachman's identity and the end of the decade, six more novels by King were published. *IT* (1986) is a long book with a complicated structure: seven main characters, in alternating story lines, face ultimate evil in the fictional Maine town of Derry in 1958, when they are children, and then return as adults to face it again in 1985. *The Tommyknockers* (1987) is a work of science fiction rather than fantasy or horror; it is about a buried alien spaceship that has eerie effects on its finders. Reviewers and critics gave this book a harsh reception, calling it sloppy, poorly constructed, and pointless. Even King's fans were generally unenthusiastic. *The Drawing of the Three* (1987), the second *Dark Tower* book, got a more positive reception. *The Eyes of the Dragon* (1987), first published in a small edition by Philtrum Press in 1984, is a fairy tale–like fantasy for younger readers. King had originally written it for his daughter, Naomi, who, unlike his two sons, did not like horror and had never read any of her father's work.

King's other two novels of the 1980s, *Misery* (1987) and *The Dark Half* (1989), explore a theme to which King has returned time and again in his fiction: the character as writer. Leading characters in *'Salem's Lot* and *The Shining* were writers, and in *Misery*, which King had originally intended to publish as a Bachman book, the writer-reader relationship is the core of the book. In *Misery* a best-selling romance novelist named Paul Sheldon has killed off his heroine, Misery, and announced plans to write a different kind of book; Sheldon hopes to write a novel that will be taken seriously by critics and will win a literary award. After an accident he is rescued by Annie Wilkes, who turns out to be his "number-one fan"—and also a "dangerously crazy" woman. Wilkes keeps Sheldon captive and forces him, through dreadful punishments, to bring Misery back to life in another book featuring the heroine.

Drawing on the power of memory and madness rather than on supernatural horrors, *Misery* is a psychological thriller that can be read as the story of a writer who is terrified of being imprisoned and diminished by his success. In an essay titled "The Rape of Constant Reader," Kathleen Margaret Lant, offering a feminist interpretation of *Misery*,

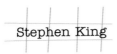

argues that the novel depicts creativity as a masculine power and uses the metaphor of sexual intercourse, even of rape, for the writer's interaction with the reader.

The Dark Half also was initially considered as a Bachman book, and it too probes into the nature of the writer-reader relationship and of artistic creativity. It is about Thad Beaumont, a writer of literary fiction who is also, under the pen name George Stark, a horror novelist. When the writer's double identity becomes public, Beaumont decides he no longer needs Stark—but Stark, the writer's "dark half," who is really the psychic residue of an unborn twin brother, has other ideas.

By the end of the 1980s, King's career had gone through several phases. He had begun by writing straightforward horror fiction, in which some terrifying or supernatural event erupts into the lives of people in a limited area. King continued to produce horror novels, such as *Pet Sematary* and *IT*. However, with *The Stand,* the *Dark Tower* series, as well as *The Talisman*, he also expanded into fantasy on an epic—even a cosmic—scale. His final publications of the decade, *Misery* and *The Dark Half*, moved into the realm of psychological suspense, a territory King explored further in future novels.

The 1980s: Screen

Many adaptations of King's work appeared on movie screens in the 1980s. King was directly involved in some of these productions, which were of mixed quality and success. King wrote the screenplays for *Creepshow* (1982); *Cat's Eye* (1985), a movie made up of three linked stories; *Silver*

Bullet (1985), based on *Cycle of the Werewolf*; *Maximum Overdrive* (1986), based on his story "Trucks"; *Creepshow 2* (1987), which King cowrote with the director George Romero; and *Pet Sematary* (1989). He also wrote two drafts of a screenplay for *Children of the Corn* (1984), which was based on a story that King had published in 1977, but they were not used in the making of the film.

King also appeared in some of these productions. He appeared in *Creepshow* as Jordy Verrill, a doltish hayseed who ends up covered with a creeping green fungus from outer space; his son Joe also had a small part in the movie. Although King did not display fine acting skills, he clearly enjoyed playing the semicomic role. He also made minor appearances in several later film and television adaptations of his work. These appearances contributed to the phenomenon of "Stephen King as a brand name." With *Maximum Overdrive*, King took on a less visible role—that of film director, a job he had not realized would be so difficult.

The other films released in the 1980s were *Cujo* (1983), *The Dead Zone* (1983), *Christine* (1983), *Firestarter* (1984), *Stand by Me* (1986), and *The Running Man* (1987). Only two of the films made in the 1980s, *Cujo* and *Stand by Me*, made King's 2009 list of his ten favorite adaptations of his work. *Stand by Me*, which was based on King's story "The Body," was directed by Rob Reiner and starred five young actors who became well known: Wil Wheaton, River Phoenix, Corey Feldman, Jerry O'Connell, and Kiefer Sutherland. Richard Dreyfuss also appeared. *Stand by Me* is a poignant coming-of-age story about friendship, family, and growing up; many critics and moviegoers consider it one of the best films made from King's work. It won Golden Globe awards for best drama and best director, as well as an Academy Award for best adapted screenplay.

Going Straight

Despite the unevenness of the film and television adaptations of his work, King apppeared to be enjoying a golden decade in the 1980s. In 1987 alone he set a publishing record with four books on the *New York Times* best-seller list at once. Behind the scenes, though, King reached a crisis. More accurately, he was pushed to it.

After years of heavy drinking, mostly beer, King finally admitted to himself that he was an alcoholic in the early 1980s. Maine passed a law allowing bottled beverage containers to be returned to stores, and the Kings started saving their bottles and cans. When King saw that four days' worth of his empty beer cans nearly filled a large bin, he acknowledged the truth. This only made him decide, however, that he had to be extra careful not to get into an accident or some other kind of drink-related trouble. In 1985 King added a cocaine addiction to the mix. His habitual use of alcohol and cocaine, along with prescription drugs such as Valium and Xanax, spiraled out of control. Blackouts became frequent. King, who was now accustomed to writing in an alcohol- and drug-induced state of mind, later said that he barely remembered writing *Cujo*. Of his work as the director of *Maximum Overdrive*, he said, "The problem with that film is that I was coked out of my mind all through its production, and I didn't know what I was doing." King denied to others that he had a problem. Tabitha, who shared the denial for a while, understood her husband's deepest fear: the fear that if he quit drinking and using drugs, if he fought off his addictions, he would find himself unable to write. By the fall of 1986, however, things had gotten very bad. King's days often ended with him passed out in a pool of vomit in his office. Tabitha knew she had to take action. She set up an intervention in which family members and friends confronted King with the evidence of his problem, a trash bag filled with liquor and beer bottles and with King's drug paraphernalia. Family members gave him an ultimatum: get straight or get out.

King decided to get straight. It did not happen at once. King struggled with sobriety for several years, but in 1988 he kicked alcohol and drugs for good. He described the effects of quitting in *On Writing*:

> I was afraid that I wouldn't be able to work
> anymore if I quite drinking and drugging, but I
> decided . . . that I would trade writing for staying
> married and watching the kids grow up. If it
> came to that.
>
> It didn't, of course. The idea that creative
> endeavor and mind-altering substances are
> intertwined is one of the great pop-intellectual
> myths of our time. . . . At the start of the road
> back I just tried to believe the people who said
> that things would get better if I gave them time
> to do so. And I never stopped writing. Some of
> the stuff that came out was tentative and flat,

but at least it was there. I buried those unhappy, lackluster pages in the bottom drawer of my desk and got on to the next project. Little by little I found the beat again, and after that I found the joy again. I came back to my family with gratitude, and back to my work with relief—I came back to it the way folks come back to a summer cottage after a long winter, checking first to make sure nothing has been stolen or broken during the cold season. Nothing had been. It was still all there, still all whole. Once the pipes were thawed out and the electricity was turned back on, everything worked fine.

The 1990s: Books

Readers of the *New Yorker*, a weekly magazine known for its literary and cultural criticism, may have been surprised when they opened the April 16, 1990, issue. There in the table of contents was the name of the world's most famous writer of horror fiction. King, a lifelong baseball fan, had helped coach his son Owen's Little League team through a championship season. "Head Down," his essay for the *New Yorker*, recounted that experience. The essay marked a breakthrough into a new market and a new audience for King. Within a few years his short fiction began appearing in the prestigious magazine.

Despite periodic rumors about his retirement, which always generated letters of protest and alarm from his fans, King was as prolific during the 1990s as he had ever been. He published twelve novels between 1990 and 1999.

In 1990 *The Stand* was republished in a "complete and uncut" edition that restored some of the 150,000 words Doubleday had made King remove before the first publication. King admitted in the preface to the new edition that many critics had regarded *The Stand* as "bloated and overlong" in its first edition (a criticism that has been frequently leveled against King's works). Nevertheless, in response to the many requests from readers over the years for the complete novel, King asked Doubleday—which still held the hardcover rights—to publish the uncut version. King updated the setting of the novel from 1980 to 1990 and added brief new sections at the beginning and end of the book. The new *Stand* was a best seller, although Doubleday had to install a special toll-free telephone number to answer questions from confused shoppers and readers who wanted to know how the two editions differed.

Next came *The Waste Lands* (1991), the third volume in the *Dark Tower* series, and *Needful Things* (1991), a tale of shopping and sorcery in which King's long-suffering fictional town of Castle Rock is all but destroyed. *Gerald's Game* (1992), like *Misery*, is a psychological rather than supernatural drama. Set almost entirely within one room, it is the story of a woman who accidentally kills her husband while she is handcuffed to a bed and must then, as she descends into self-discovery and madness, find a way to free herself or die. It was followed the next year by *Dolores Claiborne*, another psychological drama, this time told in the form of a confession by a woman who, while defending herself from the charge of murdering her employer, reveals that she murdered her husband years earlier.

Some of King's longtime fans—the loyal followers he addresses in the preface of some of his books as Constant Reader—rejected *Gerald's Game* because it dealt with the topics of sexuality and child abuse rather than with the more familiar and comfortable ghosts and demons. These fans were further dismayed by *Dolores Claiborne*; although it received many good reviews, the novel, a grim narrative about a poor, hardworking woman in a depressed environment, was a far cry from the imaginative extravaganzas many readers expected from King. *Rose Madder* (1995) also deals with the subject of domestic violence and spousal abuse, although it includes a supernatural element in the form of a painting that allows the book's heroine to enter another world.

In these psychological dramas, with their limited, almost claustrophobic settings and their focus on marital relationships, King branched out from his base. Although not all of the fans of his early genre fiction followed him, he gained many new readers who were curious to see how the King of Horror handled a different kind of subject matter. At the same time, the 1990s saw the end of the horror boom. Major authors in the field still sold well, but their works were increasingly labeled "fiction" rather than "horror," and their audiences contained more longtime fans than new readers. Meanwhile, new writers of horror and supernatural fiction failed to win mass audiences like those that had flocked to King ten or fifteen years earlier.

King's other novels of the 1990s were *Insomnia* (1994), a story of supernatural conflict set in Derry, with many connections to the *Dark Tower* saga; *Wizard and Glass* (1997), the fourth of the *Dark Tower* books; *Bag of Bones* (1998), about a writer from Derry who becomes drawn into a family tragedy in a haunted community; and *The Girl Who Loved Tom Gordon* (1999), another drama of psychological terror about a young girl who becomes lost in the Maine woods. Like Robinson Crusoe on his desert island, King's heroine must marshal her strength and her resources just to stay alive; she also has to battle what may be either hallucinations or supernatural beings.

In 1996 King experimented with what was for him a new publishing form: the serial novel. Inspired by the nineteenth-century British author Charles Dickens, most of whose enormously popular novels had been published as serials in monthly installments, King produced a novel that was first published in installments in paperback form over the course of six months. It consisted of six episodes, each of which was a complete story in itself as well as being part of an overall narrative. The stories told of a prison officer's experiences on a penitentiary's Death Row—called the Green Mile because of the color of its floor—during the Great Depression of the 1930s. The narrator, Paul Edgecombe, has an unforgettable encounter with a convicted man whose occult power is both a gift and a terrible burden. Each paperback installment became a best seller. In 2000 the six stories were published together as *The Green Mile*; a film was also made from the stories.

King resurrected his authorial alter ego, Richard Bachman, for another publishing experiment in 1996. Two closely related novels, *Desperation*, by Stephen King, and *The Regulators*, by Richard Bachman, were published at the same time that year. The link between the two novels is Tak, a malevolent force capable of possessing and destroying humans. The books place the same characters in different settings—in one book it is Nevada, in the other Ohio—and in different relationships, although they fight Tak in both books. "[The two books] were no more alike than King and Bachman themselves," King has said. "*Desperation* is about God; *The Regulators* is about TV. I guess that makes them both about higher powers, but very different ones just the same."

In addition, five collections of King's short fiction were published in the 1990s. One of the collections appeared in what was for King a new mode of publication: an audiobook. In that publication, called *Blood and Smoke* (2000), he reads stories that had not been published in print at the time; the stories appeared in print later, in 2002 in the collection *Everything's Eventual*. *Hearts in Atlantis* (1999) is a collection of five interconnected stories, also previously unpublished, about the lives of a group of people over many decades. *Hearts in Atlantis* contains some supernatural elements—many of which are connected to King's ongoing *Dark Tower* saga—but it is primarily, as many critics and readers noted, a reflection on time, memory, and the lingering effects of the choices people make. Most of the book's characters belong to King's own generation, the aging baby boomers who came of age during the Vietnam War, and in places the tone of the book is steeped in nostalgia and regret for lost time.

In the late 1990s King once again changed publishers. He felt that Viking, his publishing company for nearly twenty years, was no longer marketing his work as vigorously as it could be. In addition, he was frustrated that the company continued to view him as a horror writer, when he felt that he had moved beyond that category and wanted to be regarded as a mainstream writer who sometimes wrote horror. King's new company, Simon and Schuster, published *Bag of Bones* and the books that followed it.

The 1990s: Screen

The 1990s brought fifteen King-related films to the screen. Two were sequels to earlier films—*Carrie* and *Pet Sematary* —rather than adaptations of King's works. One, *Thinner* (1996), was based on the 1984 Bachman book of the same title. The rest of the films, with one exception, were based on stories or novels by King, although he did not write the screenplays. The one exception was *Sleepwalkers* (1992), for which King wrote an original screenplay. King also appeared in a bit part in the movie.

The best films of this era were *Misery* (1990), starring James Caan and Kathy Bates; *The Shawshank Redemption* (1994), directed by Frank Darabont and based on a King short story about freedom and friendship in prison (it received seven Academy Award nominations); *Apt Pupil* (1998), directed by Bryan Singer and based on a story about a boy who blackmails an elderly neighbor who he discovers is a Nazi war criminal; and *The Green Mile* (1999), which was directed by Darabont and stars Tom Hanks (the film received four Academy Award nominations). None of these psychological dramas can be described as a horror film, although *The Green Mile* is touched with the supernatural.

King had been lightly represented on television during the 1980s, with just a few episodes based on his work airing

In the film adaptation of *Misery*, James Caan and Kathy Bates give life to King's nightmarish vision of a writer held captive by his "number one fan."

in the series *Tales from the Darkside* and *Twilight Zone*. In the 1990s, however, King seemed to be everywhere on television. He wrote an original screenplay for the popular series *The X-Files*, although the finished episode departed from King's version. Three made-for-TV movies were based on his work: *Sometimes They Come Back* (1991), *The Langoliers* (1995), and *Trucks* (1997). The great majority of King-related programming hours, however, came in the form of six miniseries: *IT* (1990), *Golden Years* (1991), *The Tommyknockers* (1993), *The Stand* (1994), *The Shining* (1997), and *Storm of the Century* (1999). For *Golden Years* and *Storm of the Century*, he wrote the original screenplays, which were not based on any of his stories.

King also wrote the screenplay for *The Stand*. Mick Garris directed the miniseries, and King played a minor role in it. He also served as coexecutive producer, spending months at a time on the film's various location sites. "*The Stand* is like a vampire that has never wanted to lie down and be dead. And if I can live through the [production], it will be done," King told an interviewer during the filming. "People may like it, people may not like it, but it's going to be done. I think a lot of the real fans of the book are going to like it a lot. And I don't make that statement lightly." Thirty-two million viewers tuned in to the opening night of *The Stand*, and although numbers dropped over the following nights, the miniseries was regarded by King, his fans, and the executives at ABC, which broadcast the program, as a success.

Three years later ABC broadcast a miniseries based on *The Shining*. The screenplay was written by Garris, who

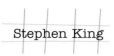

also directed; King acted as creative director for the project, hoping to produce a result that would be truer to his vision of the novel than Stanley Kubrick's earlier movie had been. While critics generally agreed that the three-part Garris-King version was well done and faithful to the novel, it failed to draw as many viewers as had tuned in to *The Stand*, perhaps because so many viewers were already familiar with the Kubrick film or perhaps because by that time King had been overexposed on television during the decade.

Life and Near-Death

Life was good for King and his family, and the Kings did good in turn. In addition to creating scholarship funds at several schools, including their alma mater, the University of Maine at Orono, they made large donations to the Bangor Public Library and paid for improvements to the local teen baseball stadium. Over time the Kings established several foundations to administer their charitable and philanthropic activities. The Barking Foundation provides money for Maine residents to go to college; the Stephen and Tabitha King Foundation offers grants to communities; and the Haven Foundation assists freelance artists who find themselves in financial distress when they are unable to work because of illness or injury. The foundations are administered by Tabitha, who has served on the directing boards of a number of social and cultural organizations. The Kings help people in other ways as well. In 2009, for example, they paid travel costs so that 150 members of the Maine Army National Guard who were stationed in Indiana could fly home for Christmas before leaving for duty in Afghanistan.

With writer Amy Tan, King takes center stage during a 1998 performance by the Rock Bottom Remainders.

King has had fun acting like a rock star in another charitable venture. Founded in 1992, the Rock Bottom Remainders is a band that includes King, playing rhythm guitar, the humorist Dave Barry, and the novelist Amy Tan. Once a year, for almost the last twenty years, the band members perform at booksellers' conventions and other events where they raise money for charity. The April 2010 "Woodstock" tour raised money for children and schools devastated by the earthquake in Haiti.

The Kings' life had its dark side, however. The family grew accustomed to fans coming to look at their house, but too-aggressive fans occasionally made the Kings feel under siege. In 1991 a man broke into the house while King was away and threatened Tabitha with a package that he said was a bomb. Tabitha fled to a neighbor's house, and when police captured the intruder in the attic of the house, they found his "bomb" was a bunch of pencils. Around the same time, a New Jersey woman named Anne Hiltner, who had sent many unpleasant letters to King, sued him for plagiarism (literary theft); she claimed that he had stolen *Misery* from her. Hiltner also accused King of basing the character of Annie Wilkes in that book on her. The suit was dismissed, but Hiltner later filed several other nuisance lawsuits. King told a radio interviewer in 2003, "I've been a lightning rod for a certain number of crazy people. . . . They feel that what I have achieved was really meant for them."

Even the man who caused King's near-fatal accident was a fan—at least of the movies. In June 1999, the Kings were at their summer home in western Maine. During King's regular four-mile afternoon walk, he was struck by a van when the driver, Bryan Smith, was distracted by his dog and veered out of his lane. Seeing the impact coming, King turned to the side; doing so probably saved his life. He recovered consciousness at the side of the road to find Smith, who had called an ambulance, sitting on a nearby rock. King later reported in a radio interview that Smith remarked, "Here it is my bad luck to hit the best-selling writer in the world." He also said to King, "I loved all your movies."

King's spine was damaged in eight places, his right hip

and four ribs were broken, one of his lungs was punctured, and he had a concussion. Most serious was the damage to his right leg, which was broken in nine places. Doctors considered amputating the leg, given the extent of the trauma, but were able to save it with a series of surgeries, after which King underwent months of physical therapy.

King, who had years earlier fought so hard to stop drinking and using drugs, now needed strong painkillers. In addition to fighting to recover strength and the use of his leg, he fought against becoming addicted. By the fall he had quit using the painkillers and had recovered enough to attend events such as movie premieres. He was also back at work—in fact, he returned to writing almost as soon as he came home from the hospital, using a little temporary office in a back hallway of the Bangor house because he was unable to go upstairs to his main office. The back hallway reminded him of the laundry room he had used as an office early in his marriage. One of the first things he did in that temporary office was finish *On Writing* (2000), a book that is part personal memoir, part writing lesson.

A New Century: New Directions

After the accident the Kings decided to spend the winter in Florida, where their daughter lived. They bought a house on the west coast of the state, and in the years to come they spent more time there, although they continued to spend their summers in Maine.

King wondered whether the time had finally come for retirement, about which he had spoken many times. He had, however, a lot of unfinished business, including a novel he had started before the accident, a commitment to write a sequel to *The Talisman* with Peter Straub, and the still-unfinished *Dark Tower* epic, which he had promised his readers he would complete. More than a sense of obligation made him want to finish the series—he cared deeply about *The Dark Tower*, which he had come to regard as one of his most important works, not simply because it is the longest and most structurally complex thing he has written, but because it gathers together many of his central themes, including the persistent presence of evil in the world; the existence of worlds or realms beyond the everyday surface of reality; the transforming power of imagination and storytelling; the value of love and life; and the nature of heroism.

A New Century: Books

King's relationship with the publishing industry and with his readers detoured briefly into new territory in 2000. A number of writers had begun bypassing traditional publishing companies and releasing their work to readers for download over the Internet, although few best-selling authors had yet ventured into direct online publishing (as opposed to offering a downloadable version of a book that had already appeared in print). King decided to give it a try with "Riding the Bullet," a short story he had written while recovering from the accident. Sold through the website of his publisher, Simon and Schuster, "Riding the Bullet" drew more than 400,000 downloads in the first twenty-four hours.

King followed "Riding the Bullet" with another online publishing venture, this time going straight to his readers. He issued six installments of a serial novel, one a month, in downloadable form from his own website. The novel was *The Plant*, a slightly revised version of the Philtrum Press tale that King had sent to friends in the early 1980s. What made the venture unusual was that King offered it to readers on the honor system. People could download the installments for free, but King asked them to send him one dollar for each download.

Although *The Plant* earned King a net profit of nearly half a million dollars, "payments fell steeply" after part 4, he reported. Although King had originally planned to continue the project with new material, he ended it after he had published the material he had already written. In 2008 "Ur," a story King wrote for the newly introduced Kindle e-reader, was published. Readers could download the story directly to the reader in digital form. Although King believes that e-publishing and eBooks will continue to change the way people read, he loves the "weight and texture" of a book in the hand. "The odor of an old book is the odor of history," he wrote after "Riding the Bullet" appeared, "and for me, the look of a new one is still the look of the future."

King's other post–2000 publications have appeared in conventional book form. *Dreamcatcher* (2001), a novel written during King's recovery from the accident, has a character who is hit by a motorist and has to deal with the aftermath of pain and recovery. The novel, which the *New York Times* critic Janet Maslin called "craftily phantasmagorical," emphasizes the struggle for survival of a band of telekinetic friends who become infected with an alien virus in the Maine woods. In this novel King made use of various elements that he had employed earlier in *Carrie*, *The Stand*, *IT*,

The Tommyknockers, and *The Girl Who Loved Tom Gordon*. That same year King and Straub published *Black House*, a sequel to *The Talisman*. The now-grown boy hero of the earlier book, who has become a detective, investigates a gruesome serial murder case that leads him on another dangerous quest through parallel worlds.

In his next novel, *From a Buick 8* (2002), King returned to the notion of a supernatural car that he had explored in *Christine*. Unlike the earlier vehicle, however, the Buick of the title does not hunt down and destroy victims. It sits in a police shed, and it is not really a Buick. It is a mysterious artifact, Lovecraftian in its strangeness, that appears to be a doorway into another world. By resisting all efforts to understand or control it, the Buick becomes a symbol of the fact that life and death are ultimately unexplainable and beyond one's control. King then turned to *The Dark Tower*. To the immense relief of his fans, who had endured a long wait after each of the first four books, King tackled the rest of the saga head-on. He had three books yet to write, and as he said in 2004, "I decided that I wanted to finish it. I wanted to be true to the 22-year-old who wanted to write the longest popular novel of all time. . . . I knew it was going to be like crossing the Atlantic in a bathtub. I thought I'm just going to keep on working, because if I stop I'll never start again." With *Wolves of the Calla* (2003), *Song of Susannah* (2004), and *The Dark Tower* (2004), King finally brought the story of the gunslinger Roland to an end.

Responses to the completion of *The Dark Tower* varied. Many critics felt that the series was uneven and likely to be fully appreciated only by hard-core fans who could keep

track of its labyrinth of plot threads and cross-references. Yet it was also, as one reviewer said, evidence of King's "prodigious skill as a storyteller." One of the most enthusiastic appraisals of the series came from Bill Sheehan in the *Washington Post*:

> On one level, the series as a whole is actually about stories, about the power of narrative to shape and color our individual lives. It is also, beneath its baroque, extravagant surface, about the things that make us human: love, loss, grief, honor, courage and hope. On a deeper level still, it is a meditation on the redemptive possibility of second chances, a subject King knows intimately. In bringing this massive project to conclusion, King has kept faith with his readers and made the best possible use of his own second chance. *The Dark Tower* is a humane, visionary epic and a true magnum opus. It will be around for a very long time.

Writing in the *New York Times*, Michael Agger disagreed with Sheehan's favorable opinion. Agger called the series a "monument to [King's] ambition" and a playground "for fantasy nerds."

King returned to nonfiction writing in the mid–2000s. In 2003 he launched a monthly column called "The Pop of King" in *Entertainment Weekly* magazine. The column, in which King offers observations and opinions on all aspects of American popular culture, showcases his genial, conversational writing style and his love of movies and books. The following year King teamed up with the novelist Stewart O'Nan, who, like King, is a passionate fan of the Boston Red Sox. The two collaborated on an account of the team's season, which ended with an event that Red Sox fans had feared would never happen: the Sox won the World Series. O'Nan and King's account, which included diary entries and e-mail exchanges over the course of the season, was published as *Faithful: Two Diehard Boston Red Sox Fans Chronicle the Historic 2004 Season*.

In 2005 *The Colorado Kid*, a mystery, was published. Although the book represented King's ongoing refusal to be pigeonholed as a writer, it used many elements that had become standard in King's fiction, including a story-within-a-story structure, old friends recalling a mysterious episode from bygone years, and a Maine setting. *The Colorado Kid* frustrated many critics because it was not a true mystery novel, much less the hard-boiled, old-school mystery suggested by the book's marketing. The central mystery is never solved, and the novel moves at a slow, conversational pace.

The two novels published in the following year represent different aspects of King as a storyteller. *Cell* is another vision of gruesome apocalypse, this time caused by a mysterious Pulse that turns cell phone users into inhuman killers; the story revolves around a father's quest to find and save his son. Horror fans welcomed King's return to more genre-related writing. *Cell* was regarded as his contribution to the popular subgenre of the zombie novel.

Lisey's Story, in contrast, is a psychological thriller that explores once again the theme of the writer whose creativity

After recovering from a near-fatal accident and overcoming addiction for the second time, King was hospitalized with pneumonia. When he learned that Tabitha had reorganized his office while he was gone, he started a story about a woman who finds secrets in the papers of her dead husband, a famous writer. The result was *Lisey's Story*, a thriller about love, death, and the power of the imagination.

comes at a price. Its main character, however, is not a writer. She is the widow of a famous writer who must deal with his unpublished papers. King got the idea when he learned that Tabitha had reorganized his office while he was hospitalized in late 2003 for pneumonia and imagined her clearing out his papers after his death. The novel that resulted was an expansion of a short story he had already written. Although *Lisey's Story* contains supernatural elements, it is primarily a love story—King wanted to write about "the world of a long marriage"—and a tribute to the beauty and fearfulness of imagination and to the power of language. Michael Chabon, an American writer who has been awarded literature's Pulitzer Prize for fiction, said of *Lisey's Story*, "King has been getting me to look at the world with terror and wonder since I was 15 years old, and I have never been more persuaded than by this book of his greatness."

Richard Bachman made a return appearance in 2007 with the publication of *Blaze*, a novel that King had written before *Carrie*, under the Bachman name. The story of a kidnapper who is a damaged man living with the legacy of horrific child abuse, *Blaze*, like all of King's books, became a best seller; King donated all profits to the Haven Foundation, founded by the Kings to help freelance writers in need.

The next year, *Duma Key* was published under King's name; it was his first novel set in Florida and his thirtieth book to reach the number-one spot on the *New York Times* best-seller list. The protagonist in *Duma Key* is Edgar, who, after being maimed in an accident that alters his personality and his very identity, becomes a painter. Artistic creation, which becomes a kind of salvation for Edgar, prevents him from committing terrible acts during fits of rage and despair, but—as is so often the case in the world of Stephen King—it carries a high cost, as his paintings begin to develop terrifying, dangerous properties. Critics noted the similarities between Edgar's accident, with its subsequent physical rehabilitation, and King's. The author acknowledged that he wanted "to write about what [a serious accident] means, how that kind of thing changes a person."

A New Century: Screen

King's work continued to be adapted for film and television. Between 2001 and 2007, six movies based on King novels or stories were released. None was a big hit, although *Secret Window* (2004) performed fairly well, largely owing to the star power of Johnny Depp. The film, based on a King story about a writer who seems to be stalked by a crazed fan or rival, has strong similarities to *The Dark Half*. The director Frank Darabont adapted an early King novella for *The Mist* (2007), the tale of a group of townspeople besieged in a grocery store by a mysterious fog. Throughout King's career he has understood that the true source of horror is fear of the unknown, fear of events or experiences that violate "normality." Still, most of his works carry seeds of hope, with survivors who remain alive to rebuild families and communities. When the movie version of *The Mist* appeared, Darabont was praised for his effective use of the mist as a source of mystery and horror, although he added a tragic twist not found in King's story.

King returned to television with the miniseries *Rose Red* (2002). During the mid–1990s King had written an original screenplay about a haunted or paranormal house as a possible movie project for the director Steven Spielberg; after his accident he expanded it to six hours for television. Critics found *Rose Red* lackluster, although audience ratings for the miniseries were respectable. *The Dead Zone*, the first drama series inspired by King's work, aired from 2002 until 2007. It was developed without any participation by King and departed in many ways from his novel and the movie that had been made from it.

Two miniseries aired in 2004. *'Salem's Lot* was an updating of the earlier miniseries; *Kingdom Hospital*, set in a haunted hospital, was a thirteen-episode production written by King and based on a Danish miniseries from 1994. King also wrote the screenplay for *Desperation* (2006), a made-for-television movie based on his novel that received mixed reviews. The *New York Times* said that the movie was "King done right" and "genuinely transfixing"; the *Washington Post* called it "an exercise in ho-hum horror" and said, "Stephen King's desperation is showing." King was not involved in the writing for *Nightmares and Dreamscapes* (2006), an eight-part series based on eight of his short stories.

Slowing Down

As Stephen King wrote his way into the new millennium, fans and critics wondered how long he would keep going. Some reviewers—even some who had enjoyed and admired his earlier work—felt that he was becoming stale and repetitive. On the evidence of *Dreamcatcher*, which he found "incomprehensible" and "flimsy," and *Black House*, which he called "an atrocious piece of work," Richard Blow declared in 2002 that it was time for King—who had recently said in an interview, "I'm done"—to retire for real.

After the publication of *Duma Key*, King said, "I think [Florida is] where pop novelists go to die, in a way. It does feel a little like retirement now, but why not. I'm 60 now, so I can kick back a little bit. Sixty's the new 50, and dead is the new alive." At the same time, however, King was working on a new book, a long novel, and later that year *Just After Sunset*, a well-reviewed volume of short stories, was pub-

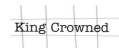

lished. The novel, titled *Under the Dome*, was released in November 2009. The story of a town mysteriously trapped in a force field, it returned to Maine, the scene of so much of King's storytelling, and to the theme of people pushed by terror and danger to reveal their true inner natures. A few reviewers noted that *Under the Dome* contains occasional clunky sentences and is extremely long—1,072 pages in hardcover. Overall, though, the novel was enthusiastically reviewed. Janet Maslin, writing in the *New York Times*, declared that *Under the Dome* "has the scope and flavor of literary Americana" and added, "Hard as this thing is to hoist, it's even harder to put down." The *Washington Post* reviewer, Graham Joyce, called *Under the Dome* "one of [King's] most powerful novels ever."

On prom night, high-school bullies drench Carrie White with pig's blood. Unfortunately for the bullies, Carrie is no ordinary teenager. Her spectacular revenge propelled *Carrie*, Stephen King's first published novel, to success in print and on the screen.

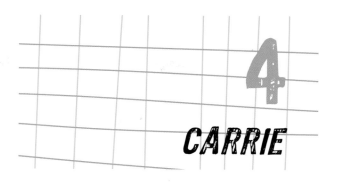

4

CARRIE

STEPHEN KING'S FIRST AND shortest novel, *Carrie* (1974), is a close-up look at coming-of-age and teenage angst. It was billed as "a novel of a girl with a frightening power," but it is not a story of supernatural horror. Carrie White's "frightening power" is explained in quasi-scientific terms. The horror in *Carrie* arises from elements that are all too real: religious fanaticism, parental abuse, and casual teenage bullying.

To develop the character of Carrie, King revealed in *On Writing,* he drew upon memories of "the two loneliest, most reviled girls" he had known in high school. One of them, "a timid and lonely outcast," grew up in an extremely strict religious household; the other encountered "ridicule and ruin" in high school because she wore the same blouse and skirt to school for a year. When she showed up in a beautiful, colorful new outfit, "[t]he teasing that day was worse than ever. . . . I saw her smile fade, the light in her eyes first dim then go out." Those memories helped create Carrie White, a character King never liked but came to understand and pity.

Plot and Characters

Carietta White, a shy, unattractive, clumsy high school senior in Chamberlain, Maine, has been a social outcast since
first grade. One day, as she showers with the other girls in
the school locker room, her first menstrual period begins.
When the other girls see the blood, they mock her and pelt
her with tampons, but Carrie is confused and terrified.
She thinks she is bleeding to death. A teacher intervenes
and learns that Carrie, who lives alone with her widowed
mother, has never been told about menstruation. Margaret
White, Carrie's mother, is an extremely strict Christian fun-
damentalist who believes that bodies are vile and that everything sexual is sinful. To Margaret, Carrie is the burden of
the sin she committed when she had sex with Carrie's father.
Carrie's life at home consists largely of prayer, beatings and
criticism, and punishment sessions in a closet for any behavior, however slight, that her mother perceives as sinful.

One of the girls who joined the mocking of Carrie in the
locker room is Sue Snell, a popular girl who barely knows
Carrie. Later, after having sex with her boyfriend, Tommy
Ross, Sue tells him that she "did a not-so-good thing today."
He advises her to apologize to Carrie. Tommy, who is a
football star and class president and as popular as Sue is, tells
Sue, "High school isn't a very important place. When you're
going you think it's a big deal, but when it's over nobody
really thinks it was great unless they're beered up." This
larger perspective is lost on Chris Hargensen, a popular
girl who was the ringleader among Carrie's persecutors.
Suspended from going to the prom for her part in the locker-
room incident, Chris vows revenge on Carrie.

Sissy Spacek portrayed Carrie White, a shy, misunderstood character based on two girls King remembered from high school. For a
brief instant Carrie blossoms into a pretty, happy teenager—and
then disaster strikes.

Carrie realizes that the strange incidents that have followed her all her life—showers of rocks on the house, bursting lightbulbs—were caused by her. On the walk home from school, she discovers that she can make things happen by "flexing" her mind. Although Carrie's mother reviles her as a witch and a "spawn of the devil," Carrie starts to feel strong as a power grows within her. Using only her thoughts, she operates a sewing machine. She believes that she can knock the door of the punishment closet right off its hinges, and she knows that her mother now thinks so, too.

As an act of atonement to Carrie, Sue Snell arranges for her boyfriend, Tommy, to take Carrie to the prom. Carrie understands Sue's motivation and accepts. Although her mother forbids her to go, Carrie defies her, sensing that her mother is now afraid of her. When her mother sees Carrie trying on the red prom dress that she has made, she tries hurting herself to get Carrie to agree not to go to the prom; she then screams at Carrie to destroy the dress: "Burn it! Burn it! *Burn it!*" Carrie tells her mother that she loves her and is sorry, but she will no longer obey; she has seen that her mother's views are warped and twisted, and she wants to make a new start in the world on her own terms.

Chris Hargensen and some of her boyfriend's older friends have planned a prank that unfolds on prom night. They arrange to have Tommy and Carrie crowned king and queen of the prom, and at the moment of Carrie's triumph, they dump two buckets full of pig's blood onto her from above. One bucket strikes Tommy and knocks him down. Carrie flees, only to return with a savage smile. In shock and

Billy and Chris, portrayed in Brian de Palma's 1976 film *Carrie* by John Travolta and Nancy Allen, scheme to humiliate Carrie. Allen has said that she did not realize during the filming how evil her character would appear in the finished movie.

outrage and humiliation, she lashes out with a power she does not yet fully understand and burns down the school; those who have not escaped are killed. Carrie then strides to town, where she ignites gas stations, makes power cables fly through the air, and creates large-scale chaos and panic. She heads home to kill her mother.

Carrie's mother is waiting with a knife and tells Carrie that she almost killed her daughter twice before, when Carrie was born and again when she was a child. Carrie says, "[I]t's not right, Momma," and begs for help and consolation. Margaret White stabs her daughter, but Carrie uses her mental power to stop her mother's heart. The wounded Carrie goes out again, finds Chris and her boyfriend, and forces their car into a fatal collision. Sue Snell, who now knows that Tommy is dead, suddenly realizes through a form of telepathic communication with Carrie that Margaret White is dead and Carrie is dying. She finds Carrie, who in a final act of destruction has destroyed the roadhouse where the pig's-blood plan took shape. Sue remains telepathically linked to Carrie's mind as Carrie cries out inside in pain, fear, and longing for her mother. As Carrie utters her last mental scream of despair, Sue feels "as if she were watching a candle flame disappear down a long black tunnel at tremendous speed," and then there is only "the blank, idiot frequency of the physical nerve endings that would take hours to die." Sue stumbles away in horror and then utters her own scream as her menstrual period begins. She is not, as she had hoped, pregnant with Tommy's child.

Structure and Style

Carrie is divided into three sections, "Blood Sport," "Prom Night," and "Wreckage." There are no chapters; each section is broken up into a number of short passages. Little more than half of the text of *Carrie* consists of scenes involving the characters. The rest is a mass of documents—newspaper bulletins, police reports, magazine articles ("We Survived the Black Prom" being one of the article titles), and extracts from a book called *My Name Is Susan Snell*. These materials provide an explanatory background—for example, one document provides information on scientific theories about telekinesis, which is the power to move objects with the mind. According to these theories, people in many cultures believe that such powers in a woman appear at menarche (the onset of menstruation); the fact that Carrie started menstruating at a late age may have given her exceptional power. Other documents reveal details about Margaret White's life and Carrie's birth and show the extent of the damage to Chamberlain on prom night.

These explanatory documents are scattered throughout the novel. The locker-room scene that marks the beginning of Carrie's ordeal, for example, is interrupted by several paragraphs about telekinesis and menstruation from a book supposedly written several years later about this so-called case of Carietta White. Readers thus know certain things well in advance of their appearance in the plot: Carrie is telekinetic; there is going to be a catastrophe; Sue Snell is going to survive. Even within the high school narrative, the reader learns of the pig's-blood plot as it forms. The suspense lies in waiting for the inevitable disaster and wondering what will happen to Carrie.

Each documentary excerpt adopts the formal characteristic of its type of publication. The scenes told from the point of view of Carrie and other characters, in contrast, are informal and intimate. King uses sentence fragments and parenthetical interruptions to show how thoughts and memories flow through scenes of action and dialogue. Tommy's death, for example, includes parenthetic samples of his own reactions to what is happening around him:

He was never even aware that something
of importance was happening. There was a
clanging, clashing noise that he associated
momentarily with
(there go the milk buckets)
a childhood memory of his Uncle Galen's
farm and then with
(somebody dropped something)
the band below him. He caught a glimpse of
Josie Vreck looking over his head
(what have i got a halo or something)
and then the quarter-full bucket of blood
struck him. The raised lip along the bottom of
the rim struck him on top of the head and
(hey that hur)
he went swiftly down into unconsciousness.

Themes and Symbolism

An obvious theme of *Carrie* is that those who are tormented may become desperate. Carrie is tormented both
at home and at school, and in her desperation she strews
havoc and destruction. She does not need to smuggle a gun
into school—she has only to unleash her thoughts. Long
before school shootings became tragically common, *Carrie*
provided a dreadful preview of what can happen when the
pressure becomes too much for a young person to bear.

Another theme—one found time and again in King's
work—is the fractured family. Not only is Carrie's father
dead, but her mother also grew up in a fatherless household.
In Carrie's case, the surviving parent is far from nurturing.

Both Sissy Spacek and Piper Laurie, who played Carrie's deranged mother, were nominated for Academy Awards for their performances in *Carrie*. Neither won, but Spacek received the National Society of Film Critics award for best actress.

Margaret White loathes herself for having once enjoyed sex with her husband, because in Margaret's mind sexual pleasure, even within marriage, is wicked. She loathes Carrie because Carrie resulted from that act. Everything Margaret says to her daughter diminishes Carrie's self-worth and confidence. Carrie and her mother live in a state of isolation. Carrie tries several times to find a place among her peers, but she only becomes the butt of their mockery, as they tease her about her mother and her religiousness. Carrie remains an outsider who cannot talk, dress, or act like everyone else.

The ambivalent power of womanhood and sexuality are central themes of *Carrie*. A girl's arrival at sexual maturity, signaled by her first menstrual period, gives her the power to create new life but carries new dangers and responsibilities. In Carrie's case that power is a source of shame that finds expression in another, more destructive power. Carrie's first stirrings of sexual feeling fuel her shame even while they make her yearn to be "normal." Two relationships in the novel show other aspects of female sexuality. For Chris Hargensen, sexual favors are leverage to get her boyfriend to do what she wants, while for Sue Snell, her sexual awakening with Tommy marks the beginning of a newly mature, compassionate identity.

Blood can be an image of life, as in birth or a blood transfusion, or of death, as in a fatal wound. In *Carrie* it always denotes death. Images of blood are everywhere in the book. A police report reveals that Margaret White gave birth to Carrie alone at home and was found in a bloody bed with the knife she used to cut Carrie's umbilical cord; readers later

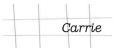

learn that Margaret meant to kill her baby but was "weak." Other images include Carrie's red prom dress and the "red plague circle" that, in Carrie's imagination, has surrounded her and set her apart from other young people since the day when she knelt to pray before lunch in grammar school, as her mother taught her to do.

The menstrual period used to be called "the curse." In the eyes of Margaret White, who has been warped by a twisted form of religion that devalues and oppresses the female sex, womanhood is a genuine curse, the mark of Satan. Carrie, for all her newfound power, cannot escape her lifelong indoctrination in her mother's beliefs. After Carrie is drenched with pig's blood, she believes that her mother was right—she *is* cursed to "final and utter ruin." The only thing she can do is "take them with her" and "cause a great burning, until the land is full of its stink."

In *The Green Mile*, set in a prison where inmates meet death by electrocution, King examined the nature of good and evil. Frank Darabont, on King's left, directed the 1999 film adaptation. Tom Hanks portrayed Paul Edgecombe, a prison superintendent who experiences mysterious and inexplicable events.

THE GREEN MILE

AFTER KING'S RISE TO SUCCESS on a tsunami of horror fiction, he broadened his approach and produced works that crossed into the territory of suspense and psychological drama. Many of these works cannot be described as horror fiction, even when they contain eerie or supernatural elements. In King's view, however, everything he has written is unified by the desire to explore what lies beyond or below the surface of life. "I'd say that what I do is like a crack in the mirror," he said in 2006:

> If you go back over the books from *Carrie* on up, what you see is an observation of ordinary middle-class American life as it's lived at the time that particular book was written. In every life you get to a point where you have to deal with something that's inexplicable to you, whether it's the doctor saying you have cancer or a prank phone call. So whether you talk about ghosts or vampires or Nazi war criminals living down the block, we're still talking about the same thing,

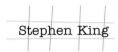

which is an intrusion of the extraordinary into ordinary life and how we deal with it. What that shows about our character and our interactions with others and the society we live in interests me a lot more than monsters and vampires and ghouls and ghosts.

The Green Mile, a novel that was published first in serial form in 1996, explores "an intrusion of the extraordinary" into Cold Mountain Penitentiary in 1932. Although the book lacks "vampires and ghouls and ghosts," it has its share of monsters—human ones—and perhaps of saints as well.

Structure

The Green Mile was published over a six-month period in the form of six short novels: *The Two Dead Girls, The Mouse on the Mile, Coffey's Hands, The Bad Death of Eduard Delacroix, Night Journey*, and *Coffey on the Mile*. In writing a serial novel, King faced the challenge of making each installment a satisfying reading experience in its own right while fitting them all together into a whole. To keep readers coming back for each new installment, he created a sympathetic narrator and a story that includes murder, miracles, and a glimpse into the mysteries of life and death. The earlier installments foreshadow events and raise questions that are not fully answered until the sixth and final book.

The narrator of *The Green Mile*, Paul Edgecombe, is the superintendent of E Block, the condemned men's cell block at Cold Mountain Penitentiary in the American South. Edgecombe oversees the Green Mile, as the convicts call the walk down the green-tiled hall to the chamber that houses Old Sparky, the prison's electric chair, and he presides over the executions.

The entire novel is told from Edgecombe's point of view; he writes the story as an old man in a nursing home looking back across a gulf of years. His narrative does not unfold in simple chronological order, however. He refers in passing to characters who are not fully introduced until later, describes events out of order, and foreshadows things he will reveal in later books. Chapter 7 of the first book, for example, begins, "Delacroix's mouse was one of God's mysteries. I never saw one in E Block before that summer, and never saw one after that fall, when Delacroix passed from our company on a hot and thundery night in October—passed from it in a manner so unspeakable that I can barely bring myself to recall it." Something terrible is foreshadowed, but Delacroix's passing does not take place until the fourth installment. (The sentence also includes two concepts that will gain importance as the novel develops: the incomprehensibility of God's will and the idea that the men of E Block, guards and convicts alike, form a "company," almost a family, united on some level

At the heart of *The Green Mile*'s mysteries are an unusual mouse known as Mr. Jingles and the hands of a drifter named John Coffey.

by their common humanity.) At the end of the following chapter, which is also the end of the first book, Edgecombe recalls a winter night when he and one of the guards made a discovery about the mouse and decided to resign from their jobs; this discovery and decision, however, took place after the events that will be described in the coming five books.

The structure of *The Green Mile* may be due in part to the circumstances in which King wrote the book. He has said that he did not know how it would end when he started it and that when the first few installments appeared, he was still writing the later ones. The organization of the first book makes clear, however, that King intended all along to present the story nonchronologically; from the beginning he weaves together scenes from different parts of 1932, as well as scenes from the year in which the elderly Edgecombe writes the narrative. This structure allows the voice of the older Edgecombe to filter into the narrative of earlier events, where it adds insight or reflection from the perspective of old age—although, as Edgecombe writes, "the order of events . . . sometimes gets confused in my head." The novel's structure also engages the reader from the start in piecing together the narrative. This engagement, along with hints and foreshadowings and the suspenseful cliffhanger endings of some of the books, gives the reader a reason to keep coming back for more of the story—a necessary condition for the successful sale of a serial novel.

Plot

The Two Dead Girls introduces key characters and sets the plot in motion. Edgecombe is a decent man doing a hard job, one that he is grateful to have "with the Depression walking around outside the prison walls like a dangerous criminal." Other characters include Warden Moores, another good man in a difficult job; Eduard Delacroix, the next convict scheduled for execution, and his unnaturally intelligent pet mouse, Mr. Jingles; and several guards, including Percy Wetmore, a vicious sadist who cannot be fired because he is related to the state governor and who will transfer to another job only after he can take part in an execution. Into this mix comes a new prisoner: John Coffey, a giant of a black man, a drifter who was found kneeling over the bodies of two little girls. Convicted of raping and murdering them, he has been sentenced to death. Coffey's mental capacity seems abnormal; Edgecombe describes him as "next door to an idiot" and says that Coffey seems lost, as though he does not know where or who he is. "In his speech as in so many other things," Edgecombe says of Coffey, "he was a mystery. Mostly it was his eyes that troubled me—a kind of peaceful absence in them, as if he were floating far, far away."

In *The Mouse on the Mile*, Edgecombe describes life in the nursing home, "as much of a killing bottle as E Block at Cold Mountain ever was." Returning to the past, Edgecombe tells how the mouse and Delacroix arrive in E Block and form a bond. Wetmore beats Delacroix and tries several times to kill Mr. Jingles. A murderer who is an American Indian is executed; the death sentence of a white murderer is commuted to life imprisonment. The warden's wife is found to have a fatal brain tumor. A violent psychopath named William Wharton is brought to E Block, breaks free, and begins strangling one of the guards. Edgecombe draws his gun.

In the third book, *Coffey's Hands*, the standoff between Wharton and Edgecombe ends when another guard clubs Wharton. Later Coffey touches Edgecombe and then exhales "a cloud of tiny black insects" (reminiscent of the wasps' nest image King used in *The Shining*) that turn white and disappear. "I slumped back against the stone side of Coffey's cell," Edgecombe says. "I remember thinking the name of the Savior—Christ, Christ, Christ, over and over, like that—and I remember thinking that the fever had driven me delirious." Coffey's touch has cured Edgecombe of a cripplingly painful infection. Edgecombe then comes to believe that although the evidence against Coffey was not ironclad, Coffey was convicted of the crime because he is black; as a newspaper reporter remarks, "[Y]our negro will bite if he gets the chance." The book ends with Wetmore stepping on and crushing Mr. Jingles.

In *The Bad Death of Eduard Delacroix*, Coffey asks Edgecombe to give him the body of the mouse, which is not quite dead. Coffey heals the mouse, to the joy of Delacroix, and once again exhales the cloud of insects. When the time comes for Delacroix's execution, Wetmore is allowed to prepare the prisoner. Just as the electric chair's switch is about to be pulled, Edgecombe realizes that Wetmore has placed a dry sponge between the cap of the machine and Delacroix's head, instead of a sponge soaked with salt water. Without the salt water to transfer electricity, the prisoner's death will be long and agonizing. Edgecombe hesitates: "[T]here was nothing I could do." The switch is thrown, and Delacroix's botched execution begins. The horror, described in graphic detail, goes on for minutes but cannot be stopped; doing so would

Who is John Coffey? *The Green Mile* offers hints, including the initials J. C., but no easy answers. For portraying Coffey, actor Michael Clarke Duncan was nominated for an Academy Award and won a Critic's Choice award.

only prolong Delacroix's agony. Delacroix finally dies. Mr. Jingles runs off and is not seen in E Block again. Wetmore agrees to transfer to a job at a mental asylum. Edgecombe, struggling with guilt over Delacroix's death, says, "We'd been part of a monstrous act, and Percy was going to get away with it . . . he would have a whole asylum filled with lunatics to practice his cruelties upon. There was nothing we could do about that, but perhaps it was not too late to wash some of the muck off our own hands." He plots with trusted guards to have Coffey cure the warden's wife.

Night Journey, the fifth book, reveals that Coffey is innocent of killing the two little girls. He was trying to revive them when he was found over their bodies. Edgecombe and the other guards know that they cannot change Coffey's fate. They smuggle Coffey to the warden's house, where the warden's wife is close to death. Coffey cures her by inhaling something out of her. This time, Coffey does not exhale the black insects.

In *Coffey on the Mile*, the final book, Coffey breathes what he had inhaled from the warden's wife into Wetmore, who shoots and kills Wharton. Wetmore then falls into a coma from which he never recovers. Edgecombe realizes that Coffey, who often knew things without being able to explain how he knew them, must have known that Wharton was the real killer of the girls. Coffey had not only cured the warden's wife but dealt out punishment to Wetmore and Wharton. When Coffey's execution is scheduled, Edgecombe and the guards wonder how they can possibly kill "a gift of God," but Coffey says he is ready to die: "I'm rightly tired of the pain I hear and feel, boss." At the end Edgecombe sees "no hope of heaven, no dawning peace" in Coffey's eyes, only "fear, misery, incompletion, and incomprehension."

The book's conclusion solves mysteries that have been hinted at throughout the novel. Edgecombe is 104 years old—although he has aged, his brief contact with Coffey has kept him healthy. Mr. Jingles is still alive, too, although he dies in the novel's final pages, a sign that Edgecombe too will die soon. Edgecombe's last words are about his wife's death years earlier in a traffic accident. As Edgecombe knelt by her body, he thought he glimpsed John Coffey or his ghost standing in the shadows weeping. Now Edgecombe is alone, waiting for his own end.

Issues and Characterization

The Green Mile addresses two social issues, racism and the death penalty. The novel's treatment of these issues emerges largely through King's use of characterization.

Edgecombe's narrative makes it clear that racial prejudice was pervasive in the American South in the 1930s. King uses the narrative to raise the question of whether things have changed since that time. Both blacks and whites are executed at Cold Mountain, however—"there was no segregation among the walking dead." All of the authority figures in the book are white, as would have been the case at the time. The plot indicates, however, that racism plays a role in the conviction of John Coffey.

Like Dick Hallorann in *The Shining*, Mother Abagail in *The Stand*, and the old guitar player Speedy Parker in *The Talisman*, Coffey is a black person who possesses special wisdom and power. He represents a type of character seen in literature for centuries. Scholars call that literary figure a holy fool—someone who is simple, naive, perhaps very young, even possibly insane or mentally challenged, but who nonetheless sees and speaks spiritual truths that are hidden from others. Yet Coffey also represents a type of character that the African-American filmmaker Spike Lee has called a "super-duper magical Negro," a black character with special powers who uses them to aid or enlighten white characters. Although Coffey and other examples of the magical Negro are honorable characters who are portrayed in a positive light, Lee and other critics have argued that this figure is offensive and limiting because it presents blacks as special and different, not fully human yet still in the service of white people. Writing in *Strange Horizons*, an online magazine devoted to fantasy and horror, Nnedi Okorafor-Mbachu points out that King's magical Negro characters "most often

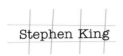

fit the stereotype of a person of color with mystical powers." She adds that while authors may mean to show respect by giving their black characters special gifts, the impression is that blacks, by being more in touch with spirits and hidden powers, are more primitive than whites.

Throughout *The Green Mile*, King emphasizes Coffey's immense size, which makes him appear threatening, and contrasts it with his gentle, even saintly nature. Coffey's initials are just one of many reminders of Jesus Christ, who also cured the sick and was executed although innocent of any wrongdoing. Edgecombe is never certain who or what Coffey is or why he possesses his miraculous powers. As for Mr. Jingles, the other character who seems to possess unusual powers, Edgecombe cannot believe the mouse is supernatural—he can only regard both mouse and man as mysteries of God.

Edgecombe is also the instrument King uses to comment upon the death penalty. Edgecombe witnesses seventy-eight executions before resigning from his job after Coffey's death. He feels that killing the condemned men serves no good purpose, but he treats them with dignity and tries to do his job with integrity. Looking back on the scene of Coffey's execution, though, the elderly Edgecombe sees with a new clarity: "Fragile as blown glass, we are, even under the best of conditions. To kill each other with gas and electricity, and in cold blood? The folly. *The horror*."

The folly and horror of capital punishment are driven home by the characters of the three men whose executions are described. Arlen Bitterbuck, an American Indian who killed a man in an argument, meets his death with grace, even dignity. Delacroix, who raped and killed a girl and then tried to destroy her body by setting a fire that killed six people, becomes a sympathetic character because of his frailty, his abuse by Wetmore, his childlike love for Mr. Jingles, and his "bad death." Coffey is saintly—and innocent. The fact that Coffey (through Wetmore) kills Wharton, the only convict with no redeeming qualities, indicates that there is a place for punishment in *The Green Mile*, even as the narrator questions the right of ordinary people to dispense it.

Themes

The issue of the death penalty is closely related to two principal themes of *The Green Mile*—that ultimate truth cannot be known and that no one is truly free.

Early in *The Two Dead Girls*, Edgecombe contemplates Delacroix and thinks that "whatever it was that had done that awful thing [the crimes] was already gone . . . [the electric chair] never burned what was inside them, and the drugs they inject them with today don't put it to sleep. It vacates, jumps to someone else, and leaves us to kill husks that aren't really alive anyway." The image of evil as an entity that exists outside human beings but can inhabit and drive them is echoed by the "black insects" of illness and death that Coffey can draw forth and dissipate. When Coffey cures the warden's wife of her fatal tumor, the house shakes, smoke rises from her bed, and something emits a shrill, animal-like scream. These images suggest that Coffey did not simply heal an organic illness but rather removed a malevolent, demonic presence.

Edgecombe says, "I believe there is good in the world,

all of it flowing in one way or another from a loving God. But I believe there's another force as well . . . and that it works consciously to bring all our decent impulses to ruin. . . . [It is a] kind of demon of discord, a prankish and stupid thing that laughs with glee when an old man sets himself on fire trying to light his pipe or ᴠhen a much-loved baby puts its first Christmas toy in its mouth and chokes to death on it." Later, having lived through events both miraculous and nightmarish and having been saved from his own death by Coffey, Edgecombe kneels at his dying wife's side and learns "a terrible thing: sometimes there is absolutely no difference at all between salvation and damnation." Coffey had saved Edgecombe from disease and given him life, but that gift was also a curse because it condemned Edgecombe to life without his wife, haunted by the memory of her dying moments.

Edgecombe's final insight, as he thinks back over the memories that have been awakened during the writing of his narrative, is that everyone's understanding is as limited

The narrator of *The Green Mile* is Paul Edgecombe as an old man, recalling long-ago events and revealing secrets. The elderly Edgecombe was played in the film by actor Dabbs Greer.

as that of John Coffey, the near-idiot. No one can truly understand innocence, evil, or God's will. Evil happens, "God *lets* it happen, and when we say 'I don't understand,' God replies, 'I don't care.'"

Just as truth and understanding are in short supply, so is freedom. The nursing home where the now-elderly Edgecombe resides is similar to the former institutional environment of his past, and not just because both are full of hopeless people waiting to die. A nursing home worker named Brad Dolan is just like Percy Wetmore: petty, vicious, and gleeful when he can perform small but nasty cruelties to those in his charge. Images of prison appear throughout the novel, although not always in a negative way. When Coffey takes the broken body of Mr. Jingles in his hands, his fingers look like "prison bars"—but within them a miracle occurs.

Edgecombe himself is a prisoner. Although he has a loving wife and a family, he spends most of his waking hours in E Block. When Delacroix stages a "circus" to show off the tricks Mr. Jingles can perform, Edgecombe, who must stage a run-through of Delacroix's coming execution, thinks, "This is the real circus right here, and we're all just a bunch of trained mice." At Delacroix's execution he is a prisoner of indecision, which prevents him from interceding while there is still time. On a larger scale, the penal, legal, and social systems pose enormous barriers to saving John Coffey.

At the end of his story, Edgecombe reveals that his long life, the gift of Coffey's hand, has become a burden. Like Coffey, he is ready to die. "We each owe a death, there are no exceptions," he writes, "I know that, but sometimes, oh God, the Green Mile is so long."

Mutilation and death by machine provide the horror in "The Mangler," an early King story. Although the film directed by Tobe Hooper changed the story considerably, victims were still sucked into a demonic laundry-folding machine.

TWO SHORT STORIES

STEPHEN KING STARTED HIS CAREER writing short stories, and he has continued to write and publish them ever since. Although he is best known for his novels, many reviewers and critics believe that some of his best writing is in his short fiction. In recognition of his mastery of that form, King was selected to be the guest editor of the collection *Best American Short Stories 2007*. Two of King's own stories—an early exercise in gruesome horror and a later, award-winning masterpiece—illustrate his range as a short story writer.

"The Mangler" (1972)

First published in the men's magazine *Cavalier* and later included in *Night Shift*, King's first short story collection, "The Mangler" was inspired in part by a man King met at his summer job in the early 1970s, when he was working at an industrial laundry. The man had lost both of his hands and forearms when they were pulled into the machine that ironed and folded the laundry, a machine known in the laundry trade as a mangle—or, as the characters in King's story call it, a mangler.

"The Mangler" opens with the arrival of a police officer named Hunton at the scene of an industrial accident: a laundry worker named Adelle has been sucked into an ironing and folding machine and killed. That night he describes the accident to his friend and neighbor Mark Jackson. They agree that the mangler's safety bar, designed to prevent such accidents, must not have been working properly. A thorough inspection by experts, however, finds nothing wrong with the machine. One of the experts, Roger Martin, tells Hunton that they do not know how the accident happened. He adds that it reminds him of an eerie incident involving an old refrigerator in which animals and a little boy had been trapped and died, and which had seemed to snap its door at a man's arm.

After another, less deadly accident on the mangler, Hunton learns that a week earlier a young laundry worker named Sherry had cut her hand, and some of her blood had spilled on the machine. Jackson suggests to Hunton that the mangler might be possessed by a demon. According to folklore, Jackson explains, demons can be cast into things by the blood of a virgin, sometimes combined with certain herbal drugs. Hunton scoffs, but after a near-fatal mangling in which a laundry worker named George loses an arm, he and Jackson make an awkward visit to Sherry, who tells them that she is a virgin. The two men talk about exorcising whatever is in the mangler. Jackson warns that doing so is dangerous—if they use the wrong method, the demon could get out. After some research, Jackson decides that they can safely handle the demon. The malevolent entity, according to what he has learned, would indeed be far too dangerous if the herbal substance belladonna had somehow gotten into the machine; he dismisses that possibility because "belladonna is definitely not indigenous to the area." Unknown to Hunton and Jackson, however, Adelle Frawley had dropped a package of her heartburn pills, which contain belladonna, into the mangler just before Sherry dripped blood on it.

Hunton and Jackson arrive at the laundry by night to perform the exorcism. To their alarm they hear the mangler running by itself in the deserted laundry. They go in and begin the ritual. It appears to be working—smoke rises from the gnashing machine. Then the mangler pulls itself free of the concrete floor "like a dinosaur trying to escape a tar pit" and opens "a gaping hungry mouth filled with steam." Hunton runs, but Jackson falls. The fleeing Hunton hears his final scream. He hurries to the home of Roger Martin, the inspector who had told him about the refrigerator, and hysterically cries that they must burn the laundry before the mangler can get out. Martin realizes that Hunton is not crazy and reaches for the telephone. Just then he hears a "steady, grinding clatter, growing louder" and smells blood as something comes closer, "gnashing and fuming." Martin's hand falls from the telephone as he realizes that the mangler is "already out."

In structural terms, the story is told primarily from Hunton's point of view. The reader sees and hears what Hunton sees and hears and also shares some of Hunton's thoughts and feelings. In several brief scenes, however, King allows the reader to see things that Hunton could not know. The scene in which the mangler seizes George's arm and a co-worker is forced to amputate it with a fire ax to save George's life is told from the coworker's point of view; a brief passage describing Adelle's loss of the pills in the mangler is told from an omniscient (all-knowing) point of view, as if by an outside observer; and the final scene at Martin's house is told from Martin's point of view.

Short stories typically focus on events involving a small cast of characters acting over a limited time. By unifying the story and allowing the reader to identify with a single character, a single point of view can increase a story's believability and intensity, and for that reason, many short story writers prefer that approach. Although "The Mangler" does not have a single point of view, however, the story is unified by other elements.

Using the technique known as foreshadowing, King builds suspense by planting hints and suggestions of what may be going to happen. The story begins, "Officer Hunton got to the laundry just as the ambulance was leaving— slowly, with no siren or flashing lights. Ominous." Later in the paragraph, the word "evil" appears. Already the ideas of ominousness and evil are present, although their cause is not yet known. Hunton walks into the laundry:

> Hunton saw it.
> The machine was still running. No one had
> shut it off. The machine he later came to
> know intimately: the Hadley-Watson Model-6
> Speed Ironer and Folder. A long and clumsy
> name. The people who worked here in the

steam and the wet had a better name for it.
The mangler.
Hunton took a long, frozen look, and then
he performed a first in his fourteen years as a
law-enforcement officer: he turned around,
put a convulsive hand to his mouth, and
threw up.

The image of the machine running when it should not be running will reappear on the night of the final confrontation. The statement that Hunton would later know the mangler "intimately" focuses the reader's attention on the machine and raises an unsettling question: will Hunton experience some kind of disaster involving it? His vomiting raises another question: Just how horrible was Adelle's death? That question is answered later, when Hunton describes the scene to Jackson: "'What I saw . . . what was left of her. . . . They took her out in a basket." As Hunton recalls the scene of Adelle's death, a description of the mechanical operation of the mangler gives way to his memories of Adelle's mangled body and "the sickening stench of hot blood," which will reappear at the end of the story.

When Martin, the inspector, tells Hunton that the mangler "seemed almost to be mocking us," the reader begins to suspect that this is no ordinary machine. Martin's anecdote about the refrigerator accomplishes two things: it foreshadows the idea that a supposedly lifeless machine may try to take lives, and it sets up Martin as the person to whom Hunton can run with his terrifying story after Jackson is killed. When Jackson warns Hunton of the possible danger of confronting the demon and then says that at least they don't have to worry about a belladonna-strengthened demon, the reader is prepared for something to go wrong. The suspense lies in wondering how wrong it will go.

King's use of language in "The Mangler" is simple, straightforward, and economical, with no unnecessary dialogue or long passages of description. In what would become a standard feature of King's style, he blends grotesque, horrific, and fanciful elements (magic and demons, the drawn-out description of George being sucked into the mangler, the comparison of the awakening mangler to a dinosaur) with the solid, matter-of-fact details of ordinary life (the details about how a mangler works, the prosaic laundromat where Hunton and Jackson discuss an exorcism with "their clothes going round and round behind the glass portholes of the coin-op washers").

From the opening of "The Mangler," the imagery King uses blurs the boundaries between animal, human, and inhuman. Readers learn in the first paragraph that Hunton had spent fourteen years "cleaning human litter" from the sites of fatal accidents and suicides. George, the man who is later mangled, is introduced as "a buffalo of a man," with an Adam's apple that moves "like a monkey on a stick." In trying to fold Adelle as if she were a sheet, the mangler seems to be destroying her human identity, even while the machine itself is likened to two living, monstrous things, a dragon and a dinosaur. As George is sucked into the mangler, his screams echo off "the steel faces of the washers, the grinning mouths of the steam presses, the vacant eyes of the industrial dryers." These images go beyond simple description to create a world in which human beings can become dead meat, no different from an animal, and a machine can come alive. Hunton accepts this formerly unbelievable truth when he and Jackson learn that the first blood spilled on the mangler was that of a virgin: "[I]n that tick of a second Hunton knew that it was all true: a devil had taken over the inanimate steel and cogs and gears of the mangler and had turned it into something with its own life."

"The Mangler" is a fast, creepy chiller. Yet woven through it are themes that appear often in King's work. One is that machines or technology may run amok, turn on human beings, and destroy or devour them. Another theme is the reality of evil. In King's world, evil is more than an abstract concept or the cruelty of humans toward each other. It is a lurking presence that can erupt into life at any time, through an ordinary object, and become both supernatural and physical. In "The Mangler" the fact that evil is a demon whose entry into the world is made possible by blood and medicine suggests that human nature and human weakness create opportunities for evil to come alive. When Hunton and Jackson talk in the laundromat, Jackson, an English professor, has a "paperback copy of Milton's collected works"; such a book would include the English poet John Milton's 1667 masterpiece, *Paradise Lost*, in which Satan and other demons are cast out of Heaven into Hell. King places his grisly tale of a murderous machine squarely in the context of the cosmic conflict between good and evil—then ends it on a note of suspense, without revealing the ultimate fate of his main character or the mangler, because that conflict is never over.

"The Man in the Black Suit" (1994)

First published in the *New Yorker* in 1994 and later included in the King anthology *Everything's Eventual*, "The Man in the Black Suit" won the 1996 O. Henry Award for best short story. In a note in the anthology, King explains that he was inspired to write the story by two things. One was a friend's anecdote about an encounter that the friend's grandfather claimed had taken place around the beginning of the twentieth century. The other was Nathaniel Hawthorne's 1835 story "Young Goodman Brown," which King calls "one of the ten best stories ever written by an American." Like the Hawthorne story, "The Man in the Black Suit" describes a mysterious encounter that flowers into doubt and despair.

At the age of ninety, Gary is writing an account of something that happened when he was nine years old and living with his parents on a farm in Maine the year after his brother, Danny, died from an allergic reaction to a bee's sting. One summer day Gary's father tells him that after he finishes his chores, he can go fishing with his new pole, but Gary must promise not to go farther into the woods than the place where the trout stream forks. Gary promises his father and his mother that he will go no farther.

When Gary sets out for the stream, he is surprised by the fact that the family dog will not accompany him. Gary enters the woods, crosses a bridge, goes down to the stream, and catches a big fish; then he moves on to "the place where the stream split in those days" and catches a smaller one. He dozes, and when he wakes, there is a bee on his nose. Terrified of being stung and dying as his brother had, Gary tries to blow the bee away. He is beginning to panic

One of Stephen King's gifts as a storyteller is the way he suggests sinister possibilities lurking in the seemingly innocent details of everyday life. The bee's sting in "The Man in the Black Suit"—is it an ordinary accident or a tool of the devil?

when a loud handclap sounds behind him. The bee falls dead. Gary turns and sees a tall man with fiery eyes in a black suit and realizes at once that the man is not human. He hopes that the man will not hurt him if he pretends not to know what the man really is.

The man sits next to Gary, who notices his long claws and his smell of sulfur. The man is the Devil, and he laughs with "the sound of a lunatic" because Gary has lost control of his bladder in fear. The Devil tells Gary that his mother has been stung by a bee. He says that Gary's mother was responsible for killing Dan because she passed on the weakness that made him allergic to the sting, and he describes her horrible death. Then the Devil says that he is hungry and is going to eat Gary; he adds that death will save Gary from a terrible motherless life with his father. To buy time, Gary offers the larger of his two fish to the Devil, who devours it and begins to cry bloody tears.

Suddenly Gary, who has been paralyzed with fright, is able to move. He runs for home with the Devil close behind. At the bridge the Devil grabs Gary's foot, but Gary throws his pole at him and breaks free. He keeps running, but when he looks back, the road is empty. Gary continues toward home and meets his father coming to fish with him. Crying, he tells his father that his mother was stung by a bee and is dead—a "man" he met told him so, he says. Gary's father reassures him that his mother is fine and suggests that Gary had a bad dream; he has had many bad dreams since Danny's death. Father and son return to the house and discover that the mother is fine. Later Gary and his father go to the stream to recover Gary's pole and creel (a basket for fish). Gary carries the family Bible with him, and although his father gives him a strange look, he does not object. Where the stream splits, they see a patch of dead, burned grass in the shape of a man. Gary's creel is empty. He tells his father that the man must have eaten both his fish. Gary's father throws the creel into the stream, saying, "It smelled bad." They do not talk about it again.

At the end of the story, Gary, old and in a nursing home, insists that the Devil was real and that "escaping him was my luck—*just* luck, and not the intercession of the God I have worshipped and sung hymns to all my life." Gary wonders if the Devil will come to him again and if he is still hungry.

The most notable structural characteristic of "The Man in the Black Suit" is the use of a framing device, two sections at the beginning and end that place the central story in context. The frame consists of short passages that show Gary as an old man recalling an event of long ago. Nine-year-old

Gary's story is sandwiched between them. This device lets King present the story through a single, unified point of view that is really two points of view—old Gary and young Gary. Young Gary describes the encounter in a vivid, direct way that includes his thoughts and conversations with other characters as they happened. Yet the voice of old Gary occasionally breaks into young Gary's narrative, as when he says, explaining why he did not try to tell his father what had really happened: "I don't think there was a nine-year-old that ever lived who would have been able to convince his father he'd seen the Devil come walking out of the woods in a black suit." These occasional comments, along with the frames at either end of the story, allow King to add a layer of interpretation, a second perspective from a mature point of view, to the central story. King employed a similar structural technique in *The Green Mile*, whose narrator, Paul Edgecombe, is also an old man living in a nursing home writing about mysterious events of many years earlier.

The opening of "The Man in the Black Suit" throws the reader back in time: "I am now a very old man and this is something which happened to me when I was very young—only nine years old. It was 1914, the summer after my brother Dan died in the west field . . ." The reader is instantly introduced not only to the story's structure but to its setting: a farm in the early years of the twentieth century. The first framing section also tells the reader that the narrator had attended the University of Maine at Orono, King's alma mater. The reader also learns that the narrator, like many of King's characters, was a writer—he wrote a column called "Long Ago and Far Away" for the Castle

Rock newspaper. The name of the column underscores the fact that the narrator is attuned to the past.

The opening section also foreshadows the kind of story Gary is going to tell. He describes the landscape of his childhood as "a different world in those days—more different than I could ever tell you." It was a lonely rural district of "woods and bog, dark long places full of moose and mosquitoes, snakes and secrets." The narrator hints at the tragedies that occur in such places when people "get a headful of bad ideas, like the farmer over in Castle Rock who had chopped up his wife and kids three winters before and then said in court that the ghosts made him do it. . . . In those days there were ghosts everywhere." The implication is that the coming story may include secrets, death, madness, and the supernatural.

The story inside the frame, brief as it is, has a three-part structure. Like many traditional fairy tales and epics, it follows a pattern called the hero's journey, in which a character is first drawn out of everyday life, then engages in a perilous quest, battle, or initiation into wisdom, and finally returns home transformed in some way. In "The Man in the Black Suit," Gary leaves his familiar life of church suppers, home-baked bread, and his mother's "housedress with little red roses all over it." On the next stage of his journey, he enters the dark forest, where he meets and escapes from the Devil; only then can he return to his home and his family. After his experience Gary possesses knowledge that he cannot share, although he does persuade his mother to resume going to church; she had stopped after Danny's death.

Gary's journey brought him a terrible wisdom, not

triumph or hope. In the closing section of the frame, the elderly Gary writes that for much of the time between that fateful day and the present, he did not even think about what had happened, and he has never told anyone about it. He then confesses that although he has led "a good, kindly life" and has no need to fear the Devil, "these thoughts have no power to ease or comfort." Sometimes, in the dark, he seems to hear the Devil's inhuman voice, "and all the truths of the moral world fall to ruin before its hunger."

Here, as elsewhere in King's work, the style of the story enhances the effect of the bizarre subject matter. By embedding the outlandish, the unreal, and the extraordinary—vampires, homicidal cars, and the Devil—firmly in the ordinary, King makes it easier for readers to accept the supernatural elements. The story has verisimilitude, meaning that the story seems true to life, and the narrator seems like a keen and reliable observer.

In "The Man in the Black Suit," King uses real-world details such as place-names (Castle Rock, Kashwakamak Township) and brand names (Serutan, Geritol, Ovaltine) to buttress the story's solidity. Most of all he uses physical description and sensory images, as in this description of the stream: "The cool rose gently off the water, and a green smell like moss. When I got to the edge of the water I only stood there for a little while, breathing deep of that mossy smell and watching the dragonflies circle and the skitterbugs skate." The images draw the reader into a scene that is reassuringly normal and matter-of-fact; when the Devil appears, the extraordinary details will be couched in similarly simple imagery.

The treatment of the figure of the Devil exemplifies King's technique of introducing supernatural elements into the natural world in such a way as to keep his stories from losing a realistic feel. The Devil is not a red, horned, caped monster—he is a man in a black suit, with a glittering watch chain and hair parted carefully on one side. Yet Gary sees at once that the Devil's eyes are "the orangey-red of flames in a woodstove. . . . He was on fire inside, and his eyes were like the little isinglass portholes you sometimes see in stove doors." Other details of the Devil's appearance also combine natural and unnatural elements, such as "slick-soled city shoes" that leave no footprints.

In addition to the theme of evil as a hungry presence in the world, themes of memory, time, and death run through the story. Old Gary's memory has become un-reliable—he cannot remember what he did yesterday or whom he might have seen in his room at the nursing home or the names of his great-grandchildren, but "the face of the man in the black suit grows ever clearer, ever closer." Long-ago events are more real to Gary than his present circum-stances: "But now I'm old," he writes at the end of the story, "and I dream awake, it seems. My infirmities have crept up like waves which will soon take a child's abandoned sand castle, and my memories have also crept up. . . ." For Gary, dream and waking, reality and imagination, past and pres-ent, now flow into one another. The reader cannot be certain that what Gary has described really happened as he says it did, and it may be that the man in the black suit, growing ever clearer and closer, is not the Devil but death, which de-vours everyone in the end.

"The Man in the Black Suit" can be read as a fable about the loss of childhood's innocence. For Gary that loss began with the shocking death of his older brother, which signaled that the safe, familiar world of home, childhood, and family life would not last forever. Gary is haunted by dreams about Danny's death until he finally accepts that bitter truth, which carries with it another truth: Gary himself will die someday. On the day of his fishing expedition, his relationship with his parents begins to change: he sees his mother for the first time "as a woman," and he feels the need to protect his father. These emotional milestones show that he is beginning to grow up. When Gary answers the Devil's greeting in a voice that sounds older than his own voice, like Danny's voice or his father's, Gary takes the first step into adult life. At the other end of that journey is old Gary, filled with dread despite his good life, because he fears that what lies ahead is not salvation but annihilation.

Tabitha and Stephen King at the National Book Awards banquet
in 2003. King's controversial literary medal hangs from the blue
ribbon around his neck.

STEPHEN KING'S PLACE IN LITERATURE

Stephen King has not attracted the scholarly criticism that the works of many of his contemporaries have done because for most of his career he has been associated with the horror genre and mass-market popular fiction rather than with what is normally considered serious literature. Still, the body of criticism that has developed examines such topics as King's relationship to literary traditions, his handling of female characters, and his use of images and settings. Not all scholars and critics feel that King's work deserves serious study, however, or that it can be considered literature. The award of a literary medal to King in 2003 sparked a debate about the boundaries of the literary canon.

Scholarship and Literary Criticism

Critical exploration of King's writing was helped along by specialty publications that either existed at the outset of his career or came into existence as he was rising to prominence. Within the large and enthusiastic genre fiction reader base were many people who wanted to read and write about the works of their favorite writers. Fanzines and genre magazines printed articles about writers and their books, and several small publishing companies formed to print critical studies of science fiction, fantasy, and horror. Starmont House, for example, was founded in 1976 and issued a number of books about King and his work during the 1980s. The early wave of King criticism came from fans, independent scholars, fellow writers, and a few academics. Douglas E. Winter, a lawyer and teacher, for example, wrote one of the first biographies of King in 1983; he also wrote a critical survey of King's early work, published three years later. George Beahm's *The Stephen King Companion* was published in 1989; Beahm wrote a number of other works about King, including *Stephen King Country* (1999), a survey of places mentioned in King's fiction.

A related development was the growth of academic interest in popular culture. In the words of the *Journal of Popular Culture*, now published at Michigan State University, "The popular culture movement was founded on the principle that the perspectives and experiences of common folk offer compelling insights into the social world. The fabric of human social life is not merely the art deemed worthy to hang in museums, the books that have won literary prizes or been named 'classics,' or the religious and social ceremonies carried out by societies' elite." On campuses and in teaching departments during the 1960s, challenges to the limitations of the traditional literary canon led to a number of innovations, such as the course in popular fiction at the University of Maine at Orono that King taught. Similar classes became part of the academic curriculum elsewhere, often joining forces with university folklore departments.

Scholars, literary critics, and graduate students began mining the rich vein of popular music, fiction, and film. Some wrote academic articles about King; chapters were devoted to his work in books on genres and themes. A 2006 volume on King in the *Modern Critical Views* series presents a selection of such articles. Among the important full-length critical studies of King are *Imagining the Worst: Stephen King and the Representation of Women* (1998), a collection of essays that examine King's work from a feminist point of view; *Dissecting Stephen King: From the Gothic to Literary Naturalism* (2006), a study of King's place within the fairy tale and other traditional literary genres; and *Hollywood's Stephen King* (2003), which uses the tools of literary criticism to analyze films based on King's work.

Additional reference works, guides, and websites are devoted to identifying and discussing the hundreds of connections and cross-references, large and small, in King's works. The character Randall Flagg, the demonic force in *The Stand*, for example, appears in *The Eyes of the Dragon*, the *Dark Tower* saga, and a number of other works. An eclipse links two of the psychological novels—King originally intended to publish *Dolores Claiborne* and *Gerald's Game* together as *In the Path of the Eclipse*, because the main characters in each book have experienced the same total eclipse of the sun, an event that created a kind of psychic bond between them. A line from an unpublished poem by King pops up in the thoughts of both Jack Torrance, the doomed father in *The Shining* (1977), and Lisey Landon, the heroine of *Lisey's Story* (2006). "The Man in the Black Suit" (1994) contains passing references to Kashwakamak Township; in

Cell (2006) a place called Kashwak in Maine plays a central role in the plot because it has no cell phone signals. Such cross-references do more than give King's followers, whom he addresses as Constant Reader, the pleasure of saying, "I know where that comes from!" They also suggest that King regards individual works as parts of a whole, an imaginative world as well as an ongoing story.

Genre Influences

Scholars have examined King's work in the light of traditional literary genres such as the fairy tale and the Gothic novel. Chelsea Quinn Yarbro, herself a writer of fantasy and horror fiction, points out in an essay on King that the classic fairy tales, such as those collected by the Brothers Grimm in Europe in the early nineteenth century, are "tales of the most dastardly, violent, despicable, treacherous behavior, and require heroic, though often unpleasant remedies." She interprets *Carrie* as a modern twist on the Cinderella story. Carrie is Cinderella, with a cruel mother instead of a stepmother and vicious schoolmates instead of sisters; the high school prom is a stand-in for the prince's ball. The twist is in the ending. Carrie not only gets the prince, she loses her life—but not before she takes revenge. "In one of the original versions of Cinderella," Yarbro says, "when she is given the chance to be revenged upon her family, she has their noses and hands cut off. Carrie goes further than that; she wrecks the entire town."

The Gothic tale is the direct ancestor of the modern story of supernatural horror, as King made clear when he wrote his own survey of the genre in *Danse Macabre*. The Gothic

Gothic fiction teems with fascinatingly evil characters such as the vampire Dracula, invented by Bram Stoker in 1897. The blood-drinking count has come to life on the movie screen many times, including this fanciful 1992 interpretation from director Francis Ford Coppola. Stephen King has studied, taught, and written about *Dracula* and the other landmarks of Gothic horror that influenced his own work.

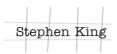
novel became popular in the eighteenth century. Many early examples, including Matthew Gregory Lewis's *The Monk* (1796), feature gloomy castles, maidens in distress, ghostly apparitions, and lurid, violent crimes. The tradition gained psychological and philosophical depth—as well as more polished writing—with works such as Mary Shelley's *Franken-stein* (1818), "The Fall of the House of Usher" (1839) and other tales by Edgar Allan Poe, Charlotte Brontë's *Jane Eyre* (1847), J. S. Le Fanu's vampire novella "Carmilla" (1872), and Bram Stoker's *Dracula* (1897). Gothic writers sought to awaken sensations of dread, terror, and suspense in their readers even when a story's supernatural elements were eventually explained as trickery (as frequently happened in many early examples of the genre) or as an aspect of the physical universe that is alien and beyond human understanding, as in H. P. Lovecraft's work.

Echoes of Gothic fiction in King's work are numerous: the vampires of *'Salem's Lot*, the haunted hotel of *The Shining*, the Frankenstein-like attempt to defy death in *Pet Sematary*, and more. In a discussion of King's literary roots, the critic Ben P. Indick points out that King's works often share key elements of the Gothic tradition, including intense emotions, "unknowable and hidden aspects of nature," and the idea that losing one's humanity—whether by being turned into a vampire, possessed by an evil spirit, or tainted by one's own bad actions—is a fate worse than death.

Loose Canon

King has described an encounter that took place in a Florida supermarket. An old woman—"I guess she's about eighty," he recalled—walked up to him and said, "I know who you are! You're that horror writer. You're Stephen King."

"Yes," King replied, "guilty as charged."

"I don't read what you do," she said. "I respect what you do, but I don't read it. Why don't you write something uplifting sometime, like that *Shawshank Redemption?*"

"I did write that," he told her.

She replied, "No you didn't."

To some people King will always be "that horror writer." He is unashamed of the genre, but he wishes that the majority of critics and scholars, the gatekeepers of the literary canon, were more willing to look beyond labels. In King's view, it is time for literary critics and literary writers to stop regarding genre writing and popular fiction as a ghetto, a vast but grimy Third World nation in the world of words, and it is also time for popular writers to stop resenting the attention and praise lavished on those writers who are perceived as more serious. He spoke about the perennial sniping between literary and popular fiction on the night he received a major award—one that had caused a stir in the literary community.

The National Book Foundation, an organization partly funded by the publishing industry, each year awards medals for the best recent work of fiction, nonfiction, poetry, and young people's literature. A fifth award is given for distinguished contribution to American letters. Although the National Book Awards are less prestigious than the Nobel or Pulitzer prizes for literature, they are meant to recognize serious work of lasting merit. In the fall of 2003, the foundation announced that the recipient of that year's

distinguished contribution medal was Stephen King.

The *New York Times* reported that Harold Bloom, a Yale University literature professor, critic, and "self-appointed custodian of the literary canon" was appalled by the award. He denied that "there [was] any literary value [in King's work] or any aesthetic accomplishment or signs of an inventive human intelligence." Bloom called the award a "terrible mistake," and "another low in the shocking process of dumbing down our cultural life." He described King as "an immensely inadequate writer" whose books "sell in the millions but do little more for humanity than keep the publishing world afloat." The former head of the company that publishes King's books said, "You put him in the company of a lot of great writers, and the one has nothing to do with the other. He sells a lot of books. But is it literature? No." Previous distinguished contribution medals have gone to some of the most respected names in American literature, including Saul Bellow, John Updike, Philip Roth, and Arthur Miller; previous winners also include Ray Bradbury (2000), a writer of fantasy and science fiction, and the television personality Oprah Winfrey (1999), who promotes reading through a book club.

King has won many other awards. He has received numerous Bram Stoker awards, which are given by the Horror Writers Association, as well as awards from the Mystery Writers of America, the Science Fiction Writers of America, and many more national and international associations devoted to genre fiction. With the exception of the 1996 O. Henry Award for best short story, however, the National Book Foundation award was the first recognition he has received from the broader community of American letters. In the speech he delivered after receiving the medal, King spoke about the split in the writing world:

> I salute the National Book Foundation Board, who took a huge risk in giving this award to a man many people see as a rich hack. For far too long the so-called popular writers of this country and the so-called literary writers have stared at each other with animosity and a willful lack of understanding. . . . But giving an award like this to a guy like me suggests that in the future things don't have to be the way they've always been. Bridges can be built between the so-called popular fiction and the so-called literary fiction. The first gainers in such a widening of interest would be the readers, of course.

Both Sides of the Bridge?

By the time King won the National Book Foundation award in 2003, his reign as the king of best-selling authors was drawing to an end, at least in terms of numbers. His books regularly made the *New York Times* best-seller list and sometimes topped it, but now they stayed there for a few weeks, rather than for months at a time as they had once done. Horror fiction in general had experienced a decline in sales during the 1990s, and although the genre revived in the 2000s, King's fan base had eroded somewhat. At the same time, although King's work had become more varied and harder to classify as horror, he had not attracted large numbers of new readers.

King acknowledged in a 2006 interview with the literary magazine *Paris Review* that he had reached the point of being outsold by other big-name authors but added, "It's not a big deal to me anymore." What King had lost in sales numbers was perhaps offset by rising respect in the literary world. Some critics clearly felt the one-time King of Horror had earned the right to be taken seriously as a writer, plain and simple—a writer with one foot on either side of the bridge between popular and literary fiction.

The critic Leslie Fiedler, known for his interest in popular and genre fiction as well as in such mainstays of American literature as Nathaniel Hawthorne, F. Scott Fitzgerald, and Ernest Hemingway, said in early 2003, "Stephen King really fascinates me"; he called King "a secret intellectual." Fiedler predicted that King would be read and remembered long into the future. A few years later the *Washington Post* declared, "With *Lisey's Story*, King has crashed the exclusive party of literary fiction, and he'll be no easier to ignore than Carrie at the prom."

In the view of columnist and critic Ross Douthat, King does not so much bridge the gap between popular and literary fiction as stand in "a gray zone between the pulpy authors who can match his sales figures—the Dan Browns and the Danielle Steeles—and the literary authors whose company he obviously craves, the writers who stand a chance of winning, not a lifetime achievement medal, but the actual National Book Award itself." Douthat argued in 2007 that whatever King's literary weaknesses, the author's great achievement has been to fuse the natural, everyday world of American families and their culture with an awareness that

A fan's devotion is rewarded with a hug from the author. Stephen King has inspired scorn from some critics, but he has also won the affectionate loyalty of millions of those he calls his "constant readers."

the supernatural realm—and therefore the spiritual dimension of life—are always with us.

Perhaps if Stephen King had not begun his career with such spectacular success in the horror genre, or had written fewer books, he would be taken more seriously by more critics—and by more readers like the woman in that Florida supermarket. Yet King has always written what he wanted to write, or felt compelled to write, driven as much by the need to test himself on the page and reach readers as by the desire to achieve record-breaking success.

The sheer size of King's output, and the grand scale of his record-breaking achievements as a writer, are unmistakable, as is his commitment to his work. In a 1996 review of *The Green Mile*, Bruce Handy pointed out that King had published "1,755 pages of fiction in less than 12 months" and asked, "Is there such a thing as writer's unblock?" Handy acknowledged the essential sincerity of King's work in concluding that *"The Green Mile* has the courage of its cornier convictions. You might even say the palpable sense of King's sheer, unwavering belief in his tale is what makes the novel work as well as it finally does. Or maybe it is the palpable sense of his sheer need to write."

King's own evaluations of his career are typically delivered in low-key, straightforward language. "Being a brand name is all right. Trying to be a writer, trying to fill the blank sheet in an honorable and truthful way, is better," he once wrote. In 2003, after winning the National Book Foundation award, he said, "I've never denied that I was a horror writer, but I've never introduced myself as that either. I see myself as Stephen King. I'm an American novelist, and that's it."

WORKS

Dates are for first professional publication of a story, collection, novel, nonfiction book, or comic.

Short Stories, Novellas, and Poems

1967 "The Glass Floor"

1968 "Cain Rose Up"
"Here There Be Tygers"

1969 "The Reaper's Image"

1970 "Graveyard Shift"

1971 "I Am the Doorway"

1972 "Battleground"
"The Fifth Quarter" (written as John Swithen)
"The Mangler"
"Suffer the Little Children"

1973 "Gray Matter"
"Trucks"
"The Boogeyman"

1974 "Sometimes They Come Back"
"Night Surf"

1975 "It Grows on You"
"The Lawnmower Man"
"Strawberry Spring"

1976 "I Know What You Need"

"The Ledge"

"Weeds"

1977 "The Cat from Hell"

"Children of the Corn"

"The Man Who Loved Flowers"

"One for the Road"

1978 "Jerusalem's Lot"

"The Gunslinger"

"The Last Rung on the Ladder"

"Nona"

"Man with a Belly"

"Quitters, Inc."

"The Night of the Tiger"

"The Woman in the Room"

1979 "The Crate"

1980 "Crouch End"

"The Mist"

"The Monkey"

"The Way Station"

"The Wedding Gig"

1981 "The Bird and the Album"

"The Jaunt"

"Monster in the Closet"

"The Oracle and the Mountains"

"The Reach" (also published as "Do the Dead Sing?")

"The Slow Mutants"

"The Gunslinger and the Dark Man"

1982 "The Man Who Would Not Shake Hands"

"Apt Pupil"

"Before the Play"

"Big Wheels: A Tale of the Laundry Game
(Milkman #2)"
"The Body"
"The Breathing Method"
"The Raft"
"Rita Hayworth and the Shawshank Redemption"
"Survivor Type"
1983   "The Return of Timmy Baterman"
"Uncle Otto's Truck"
"Word Processor of the Gods"
1984   "The Ballad of the Flexible Bullet"
"Beachworld"
"Gramma"
"Mrs. Todd's Shortcut"
"The Revelations of 'Becka Paulson"
1985   "Dolan's Cadillac"
"Morning Deliveries (Milkman #1)"
"For Owen"
"Paranoid: A Chant"
1986   "The End of the Whole Mess"
1987   "The Doctor's Case"
"Popsy"
1988   "Dedication"
"The Night Flier"
"The Reploids"
"Sneakers"
1989   "Home Delivery"
"My Pretty Pony"
"Rainy Season"
1990   "The Langoliers"

"The Library Policeman"
"The Moving Finger"
"Secret Window, Secret Garden"
"The Sun Dog"
1992 "Chattery Teeth"
"You Know They Got a Hell of a Band"
1993 "Jhonathan and the Witchs"
"The Beggar and the Diamond"
"The House on Maple Street"
"The Ten O'Clock People"
"Umney's Last Case"
"Sorry, Right Number"
"Brooklyn August"
1994 "Blind Willie"
"The Killer"
"The Man in the Black Suit"
1995 "Luckey Quarter"
"Lunch at the Gotham Cafe"
1997 "Autopsy Room Four"
"Everything's Eventual"
"L.T.'s Theory of Pets"
1998 "The Little Sisters of Eluria"
"That Feeling, You Can Only Say What It Is in French"
1999 "1408"
"The New Lieutenant's Rap"
"Low Men in Yellow Coats"
"Hearts in Atlantis"
"Why We're in Vietnam"
"Heavenly Shades of Night Are Falling"
"In the Deathroom"

"The Road Virus Heads North"

2000 "The Old Dude's Ticker"

"Riding the Bullet"

2001 "All That You Love Will be Carried Away"

"Calla Bryn Sturgis"

"The Death of Jack Hamilton"

2003 "Harvey's Dream"

"Rest Stop"

"Stationary Bike"

"The Tale of Gray Dick"

2005 "The Furnace" (King wrote first two paragraphs)

"The Things They Left Behind"

2006 "Memory"

"Willa"

2007 "Mute"

"Ayana"

"The Cat from Hell"

"The Gingerbread Girl"

"Graduation Afternoon"

2008 "N."

"The New York Times at Special Bargain Rates"

"A Very Tight Place"

2009 "Ur"

"Morality"

"Throttle" (written with Joe Hill)

Collections

Night Shift (1978)

Different Seasons (1982)

Skeleton Crew (1985)

Four Past Midnight (1990)
Nightmares and Dreamscapes (1993)
Six Stories (1997)
Hearts in Atlantis (1999)
Blood and Smoke (audiobook) (2000)
Everything's Eventual (2002)
The Secretary of Dreams (2006)
Just after Sunset (2008)
Stephen King Goes to the Movies (2009)

Novels
Carrie (1974)
'Salem's Lot (1975)
The Shining (1977)
Rage (written as Richard Bachman) (1977)
The Stand (1978)
The Dead Zone (1979)
The Long Walk (written as Richard Bachman) (1979)
Firestarter (1980)
Cujo (1981)
Roadwork (written as Richard Bachman) (1981)
The Running Man (written as Richard Bachman) (1982)
The Gunslinger (*The Dark Tower I*) (1982)
Christine (1983)
Pet Sematary (1983)
Cycle of the Werewolf (1983)
The Talisman (written with Peter Straub) (1984)
Thinner (written as Richard Bachman) (1984)
IT (1986)
The Eyes of the Dragon (1987)

The Tommyknockers (1987)

The Drawing of the Three (*The Dark Tower II*) (1987)

Misery (1987)

The Dark Half (1989)

The Stand: Complete and Uncut Edition (1990)

The Waste Lands (*The Dark Tower III*) (1991)

Needful Things (1991)

Gerald's Game (1992)

Dolores Claiborne (1993)

Insomnia (1994)

Rose Madder (1995)

The Two Dead Girls (1996)

The Mouse on the Mile (1996)

Coffey's Hands (1996)

The Bad Death of Eduard Delacroix (1996)

Night Journey (1996)

Coffey on the Mile (1996)

Desperation (1996)

The Regulators (written as Richard Bachman) (1996)

Wizard and Glass (*The Dark Tower IV*) (1997)

Bag of Bones (1998)

The Girl Who Loved Tom Gordon (1999)

The Green Mile (2000)

The Plant: Zenith Rising (six installments published online; book never finished) (2000)

Dreamcatcher (2001)

Black House (written with Peter Straub) (2001)

From a Buick 8 (2002)

Wolves of the Calla (*The Dark Tower V*) (2003)

Song of Susannah (*The Dark Tower VI*) (2004)

The Dark Tower (*The Dark Tower VII*) (2004)
The Colorado Kid (2005)
Lisey's Story (2006)
Cell (2006)
Blaze (written as Richard Bachman) (2007)
Duma Key (2008)
Under the Dome (2009)

Nonfiction

Danse Macabre (1981)
Nightmares in the Sky (book of photographs with text by King) (1988)
Mid-Life Confidential: The Rock Bottom Remainders Tour America with Three Chords and an Attitude (King contributed to this group-written work) (1994)
On Writing: A Memoir of the Craft (2000)
Secret Windows: Essays and Fiction on the Craft of Writing (2000)
Faithful (written with Stewart O'Nan) (2004)

Comics and Graphic Novels

Bizarre Adventures #29 (1981)
Creepshow (1982)
The Dark Tower: The Gunslinger Born (2007)
The Dark Tower: The Long Road Home (2008)
The Dark Tower: Treachery (2008)
The Stand: Captain Trips (2008)
The Dark Tower: Sorcerer (2009)
The Dark Tower: Fall of Gilead (2009)
The Stand: American Nightmares (2009)

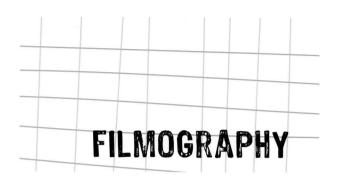

FILMOGRAPHY

Films

Carrie (1976)

The Shining (1980)

Creepshow (1982)

Cujo (1983)

The Dead Zone (1983)

Christine (1983)

Firestarter (1984)

Children of the Corn (1984)

Cat's Eye (1985)

Silver Bullet (1985)

Maximum Overdrive (1986)

Stand by Me (1986)

Creepshow 2 (1987)

The Running Man (1987)

Pet Sematary (1989)

Tales from the Darkside (1990)

Graveyard Shift (1990)

Misery (1990)

Sleepwalkers (1992)

The Dark Half (1993)
Needful Things (1993)
The Shawshank Redemption (1994)
The Mangler (1995)
Dolores Claiborne (1995)
Thinner (1996)
The Night Flier (1997)
Apt Pupil (1998)
The Green Mile (1999)
Hearts in Atlantis (2001)
Dreamcatcher (2003)
Secret Window (2004)
Riding the Bullet (2004)
1408 (2007)
The Mist (2007)

Television

Salem's Lot (1979)
Tales from the Darkside: "Word Processor of the Gods" (1984)
Twilight Zone: "Gramma" (1986)
Tales from the Darkside: "Sorry, Right Number" (1987)
It (1990)
Monsters: "The Moving Finger" (1990)
Sometimes They Come Back (1991)
Golden Years (1991)
The Tommyknockers (1993)
The Stand (1994)
The Langoliers (1995)
Trucks (1997)

The Shining (1997)

Quicksilver Highway: "Chattery Teeth" (1997)

The Outer Limits: "The Revelations of 'Becka Paulson" (1997)

The X-Files: "Chinga" (1998)

Storm of the Century (1999)

Rose Red (2002)

Carrie (2002)

The Dead Zone (2002–2007)

Kingdom Hospital (2004)

'Salem's Lot (2004)

Desperation (2006)

Nightmares and Dreamscapes (2006)

CHRONOLOGY

Only a few of King's book publications are cited in this section. A complete list of his works with their dates of publication is on pages 139–149.

1939
Donald Edwin King and Nellie Ruth Pillsbury marry in Scarborough, Maine

1945
The Kings adopt a baby boy, David Victor

1947
Stephen Edwin King is born on September 21 in Portland, Maine

1949
Donald King abandons his wife and two sons; they never see him again

1958
Stephen King, his mother, and his brother move to Durham, Maine

1965
While in high school, King publishes his first short story

1966–1970

Attends the University of Maine at Orono (UMO)

1967

In his first literary sale, is paid thirty-five dollars for a short story called "The Glass Floor"

1969

Meets a fellow UMO student, Tabitha Spruce

1970

Their daughter, Naomi, is born

1971

King marries Spruce; begins teaching English

1972

A son, Joseph, is born; King begins writing *Carrie*

1973

Sells *Carrie*; quits his teaching job to write full-time; completes the novel later known as *'Salem's Lot* (published in 1975)

1974

Carrie is published; King moves to Colorado; begins *The Shining* and *The Stand*

1975

Returns to Maine

1976

The film adaptation of *Carrie* is released

1977

A son, Owen, is born; King and his family move temporarily to England, where he begins writing *The Dead Zone* and *Firestarter*; *Rage* is published under the pen name Richard Bachman

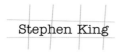
1978–1979

King teaches at his alma mater, the University of Maine at Orono

1980

Buys an old house in Bangor, Maine; begins donating his papers to UMO

1982

The Gunslinger, the first *Dark Tower* novel, is published

1984

The Talisman, written with Peter Straub, is published

1985

King reveals that he is Richard Bachman, the author of five published novels

1986

Decides to end alcohol and drug use

1990

"Head Down," King's essay about the Maine Little League championship won by his son Owen's team, appears in the *New Yorker*; *The Stand* is reissued in a complete edition

1991

An intruder breaks into the Kings' home in Bangor

1992

King joins the Rock Bottom Remainders, a part-time rock band whose members are writers

1996

Wins the O. Henry Award for short fiction (for "The Man in the Black Suit")

1999

While out walking, is severely injured on June 19 when he is struck by a van

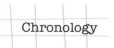

2001

Black House, the second collaboration with Peter Straub, is published

2002

King wins the lifetime achievement award from the Horror Writers Association

2003

Receives the National Book Foundation's Medal for Distinguished Contribution to American Letters (the National Book Award)

2004

The final two volumes of the seven-volume *Dark Tower* series are published; King coauthors *Faithful*, a nonfiction book about the World Series–winning 2004 Boston Red Sox

2005

The Colorado Kid, a mystery novel, is published

2007

With Richard Bachman as author, *Blaze*, revised from a 1973 draft, is published; King receives a grand master award from the Mystery Writers of America

2008

Duma Key and the short-story collection *Just after Sunset* are published

2009

Under the Dome is published

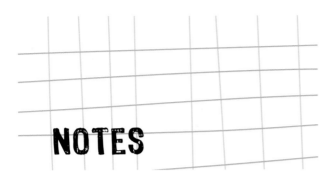

NOTES

Throughout the manuscript, all references to Stephen King's works refer to the following editions of his works:

Stephen King, *Carrie*, New York: Plume, 1991.
Stephen King, *Danse Macabre*, New York: Berkley, 1983.
Stephen King, *The Green Mile*, New York: Scribner, 2000.
Stephen King, "The Mangler," *Night Shift*, New York: Doubleday, 1978.
Stephen King, "The Man in the Black Suit," *Everything's Eventual*, New York: Scribner, 2002.
Stephen King, *On Writing*, New York: Pocket Books, 2001.

Introduction
p. 8: "more number-one best-selling books. . .": Hawes Publications, "New York Times Bestseller Listings," www.hawes.com/pastlist.htm (accessed February 4, 2010).

Chapter One
pp. 11–12: "chicken skeletons . . .": Stephen King, *Danse Macabre*, 94.

p. 13: "treasure trove . . .": Stephen King, *Danse Macabre*, 95.

p. 14: "a man with an itchy foot . . .": Stephen King, quoted in Lisa Rogak, *Haunted Heart: The Life and Times of Stephen King*, New York: Saint Martin's Press, 2008, 10.

p. 14: "no memory of his father . . .": Tim Adams, "The Stephen King Interview," *Guardian*, United Kingdom, September 14, 2000, www.guardian.co.uk/books/2000/sep/14/stephenking.fiction (accessed February 4, 2010).

p. 15: "four families and a graveyard . . .": Rogak, *Haunted Heart*, 19.

p. 16: "We were ashamed . . .": Adams, "The Stephen King Interview," September 14, 2000.

p. 16: "The issue of his father's abandonment . . .": Michael Collings, quoted in Rogak, *Haunted Heart*, 124.

p. 17: "I *liked* to be scared . . .": King, quoted in Rogak, *Haunted Heart*, 16.

p. 21: "War on Poverty . . .": King, *On Writing*, 58.

p. 22: "He was the biggest kid . . .": Rogak, *Haunted Heart*, 27.

p. 22: "junk like this . . .": King, *On Writing*, 49.

p. 25: "It wasn't the best summer . . .": King, *On Writing*, 59.

Chapter Two

p. 27: "I was made to write stories . . .": Stephen King, "Frequently Asked Questions," StephenKing.com, www.stephenking.com/faq.html#1.0 (accessed January 29, 2010).

p. 30: "dead white males . . .": Paul Gray, "Hurrah for Dead White Males!" *Time*, October 10, 1994, www.time.com/time/magazine/article/0,9171,981571,00.html (accessed February 4, 2010).

p. 34: "my ideal reader . . .": Jill Owens, "The Once and Future King," Powell's City of Books, 2006, www.powells.com/authors/stephenking.html (accessed January 29, 2010).

p. 34: "You've got something here . . .": King, *On Writing*, 77.

p. 35: "put Durham on the map . . .": David Bright, "Hampden Teacher Hits Jackpot with New Book," *Bangor Daily News*, May 25, 1973, quoted in Tim Underwood and Chuck Miller, *Feast of Fear: Conversations with Stephen King*, eds., New York: Carroll and Graf, 1989, 1–3.

p. 36: "There are so many small towns . . .": Stephen King, "On Becoming a Brand Name," in *Adelina*, February 1980, 44, quoted in Douglas E. Winter, *The Art of Darkness*, New York: New American Library, 41.

p. 37: "one of the things . . .": Leonard Wolf, *Dracula: The Connoisseur's Guide*, New York: Broadway Books, 1997, 185, quoted in George Beahm, *Stephen King: America's Best-Loved Boogeyman*, Kansas City, MO: Andrews McMeel, 1998, 38.

p. 37: "King's Maine . . .": Tony Magistrale, *Landscape of Fear: Stephen King's American Gothic*, Madison: University of Wisconsin Popular Press, 1988, 18–19.

p. 38: "an inventive, rich novel . . .": George Beahm, *Stephen King: America's Best-Loved Boogeyman*, Kansas City, MO: Andrews McMeel, 1998, 35.

p. 39: "chilling moments . . .": Jack Sullivan, "The Shining," *New York Times*, February 20, 1977.

p. 40: "core of psychological truth . . .": Richard R. Lingeman, "Something Nasty in the Tub," *New York Times*, March 1, 1977.

p. 42: "It's a long way from teaching . . .": Emmett Meara, "Stephen King's Silver-Lined Prose," *Bangor Daily News*, February 12, 1977, quoted in Underwood and Miller, eds., *Feast of Fear*, 5.

p. 43: For further discussion of films based on King's work, *see*: Tony Magistrale, *Hollywood's Stephen King*, New York: Palgrave Macmillan, 2003.

p. 44: "nothing in the movie is really scary . . .": Craig Modderno, "Topic: Horrors!" *USA Today*, May 10, 1985, quoted in Tim Underwood and Chuck Miller, eds., *Bare Bones: Conversations with Stephen King*, New York: Warner, 1988, 143.

p. 44: "We didn't feel comfortable . . .": Stephen King, quoted in Lisa Rogak, *Haunted Heart: The Life and Times of Stephen King*, New York: Saint Martin's Press, 2008, 80.

p. 45: "the land of the ghost story . . .": Stephen King, *An Audience with Stephen King*, BBC, November 12, 2006, quoted in Rogak, *Haunted Heart,* 90.

p. 46: "I think that you can teach writers . . .": Paul Janeczko, "An Interview with Stephen King," *English Journal*, February 1980, quoted in Underwood and Miller, eds., *Bare Bones*, 76.

Chapter Three

p. 51: "The bottom line . . .": Edgar Allen Beem, "Midas with the Common Touch: Why Hasn't Success Spoiled Stephen King?," *Maine Times*, July 11, 1986, quoted in Tim Underwood and Chuck Miller, eds., *Feast of Fear: Conversations with Stephen King*, New York: Carroll and Graf, 1989, 276.

p. 54: For further discussion of *Pet Sematary*, *see*: Christopher Lehmann-Haupt, Review of *Pet Sematary*, *New York Times*, October 21, 1983, C31; Mary Chelton, Review of *Pet Sematary*, *Voice of Youth Advocates*, April 1984, 32.

p. 55: "a good voice . . .": Stephen King, "The Importance of Being Bachman," Lilja's Library, www.liljas-library.com/bachman_king. php (accessed January 29, 2010).

p. 56: "[Bachman] is not good King . . .": Everett F. Bleiler, "The Ghosts of Christmas Present," *Washington Post*, December 23, 1984, 11.

p. 56: "written with verve . . .": S. T. Joshi, *The Modern Weird Tale*, Jefferson, NC: McFarland, 2001, 64.

p. 56: "King withdrew that book [*Rage*] . . ." Stephen King, "The Bogeyboys," Keynote Address, Vermont Library Conference, Killington, VT, May 26, 1999, www.horrorking.com/interview7.html (accessed February 4, 2010).

p. 58: For further discussion of the metaphor of sexual intercourse, *see*: Kathleen Margaret Lant, "The Rape of Constant Reader: Stephen King's Construction of the Female Reader and Violation of the Female Body in *Misery*," *Journal of Popular Culture*, 1997, 30.

p. 59: "a job he had not realized would be so difficult . . .": Tim Underwood and Chuck Miller, *Feast of Fear: Conversations with Stephen King*, New York: Carroll and Graf, 1989.

p. 59: "his ten favorite adaptations of his work . . .": Stephen King, *Stephen King Goes to the Movies*, New York: Pocket Books, 2009, 627.

p. 60: "The problem with that film . . .": Stephen King, quoted in Lisa Rogak, *Haunted Heart: The Life and Times of Stephen King*, New York: Saint Martin's Press, 2008, 142.

p. 66: "*Desperation* is about God . . ." Stephen King, "The Importance of Being Bachman."

p. 69: "People may like it . . .": Bruce Fretts, "King of the Road," *Entertainment Weekly*, May 6, 1994, www.ew.com/ew/article/0302101,00.html (accessed January 29, 2010).

p. 70: "In 2009, for example, they paid travel . . .": Associated Press, "Stephen King to Pay for Troops' Holiday Trip Home," *Salon.com*, December 12, 2009, www.salon.com/books/story/index.html?story=/books/2009/12/12/us_people_stephen_king_troops (accessed January 29, 2010).

p. 72: "I've been a lightning rod . . .": Stephen King, *Fresh Air from WHYY*, National Public Radio, November 21, 2003.

p. 72: "Here it is my bad luck . . .": Stephen King, *Fresh Air from WHYY*, National Public Radio, October 10, 2000.

p. 75: "payments fell steeply . . .": Stephen King, "How I Got That Story," *Time*, December 18, 2000, www.time.com/time/magazine/article/0,9171,998828-2,00.html (accessed January 29, 2010).

p. 75: "The odor of an old book . . .": Stephen King, "Will We Close the Book on Books?" *Time*, June 19, 2000, www.time.com/time/magazine/article/0,9171,997272,00.html (accessed January 29, 2010).

p. 76: "life and death are ultimately unexplainable . . .": Laura Miller, "Imagining Death," *Salon.com*, September 9, 2002, http://dir.salon.com/story/books/feature/2002/09/09/fiction/index.html (accessed February 4, 2010).

p. 76: "I decided that I wanted to finish it . . .": Stuart Jeffries, "Dark Rider," *Guardian*, September 18, 2004, www.guardian.co.uk/books/2004/sep/18/stephenking.featuresreviews (accessed January 29, 2010).

p. 77: "prodigious skill as a storyteller . . .": Michael Berry, "Waiting for the End of Their Worlds," *San Francisco Chronicle*, September 26, 2004, www.sfgate.com/cgi-bin/article.cgi?f=/c/a/2004/09/26/RVGR98QA141.DTL (accessed January 29, 2010).

p. 77: "On one level . . .": Bill Sheehan, "The Return of the King," *Washington Post*, September 19, 2004, www.washingtonpost.com/ac2/wp-dyn?pagename=article&node=&contentId=A27485-2004Sep16 (accessed January 29, 2010).

p. 77: "fantasy nerds . . .": Michael Agger, "'The Dark Tower:' Pulp Metafiction," *New York Times*, October 17, 2004, www.nytimes.com/2004/10/17/books/review/17AGGERL.html?page

wanted=1&ei=5090&en=c3b0bc5048e91c68&ex=1255665600&par
tner=rssuserland (accessed January 29, 2010).

p. 80: "the world of a long marriage . . .": Jill Owens, "The Once
and Future King," Powell's City of Books, 2006, www.powells.
com/authors/stephenking.html (accessed January 29, 2010).

p. 80: "King has been getting me to look at the world . . .": Review
of *Lisey's Story*, by Stephen King, *Kirkus Review: Autumn & Winter
Preview 2006*, 8, www.kirkusreviews.com/kirkusreviews/images/
pdf/Kirkus_Aut_Win_preview_8.06.pdf (accessed January 29,
2010).

p. 80: "changes a person . . .": Gilbert Cruz, "King's New
Realm," *Time*, January 17, 2008, www.time.com/time/magazine/
article/0,9171,1704697,00.html (accessed January 29, 2010).

p. 81: "When the movie version of *The Mist* . . .": Manohla
Dargis, "Something Creepy This Way Comes, and It Spells Bad
News," *New York Times*, November 21, 2007, movies.nytimes.
com/2007/11/21/movies/21mist.html (accessed January 29, 2010).

p. 82: "Stephen King's desperation is showing": Tom Shales,
"Stephen King Mines That Tapped-Out Vein," *Washington Post*,
May 23, 2006.

p. 82: "an atrocious piece of work . . .": Richard Blow, "The Chill
Is Gone," *Salon.com*, February 19, 2002, http://dir.salon.com/
story/books/feature/2002/02/19/king_retire/index.html (accessed
January 29, 2010).

p. 82: "dead is the new alive . . .": Gilbert Cruz, "King's New
Realm," *Time*, January 17, 2008.

p. 83: For further discussion of *Under the Dome*, *see*: Janet Maslin,
"Stephen King's Latest Cast Feels Real," *New York Times*, November 11, 2009, www.nytimes.com/2009/11/12/books/12book.html
(accessed January 29, 2010).

Chapter Five

p. 97: "If you go back over the books . . .": Nathaniel Rich, "Interview with Stephen King," *Paris Review*, 178, Fall 2006, http://theparisreview.org/viewinterview.php/prmMID/5653 (accessed January 29, 2010).

p. 105: "magical Negro . . .": Susan Gonzalez, "Director Spike Lee Slams 'Same Old' Black Stereotypes in Today's Films," *Yale Bulletin & Calendar*, 29, 21, March 2, 2001, www.yale.edu/opa/arc-ybc/v29.n21/story3.html (accessed January 29, 2010).

pp. 105–106: "a person of color with mystical powers . . .": Nnedi Okorafor-Mbachu, "Stephen King's Super-Duper Magical Negroes," *Strange Horizons*, October 24, 2004, http://www.strange horizons.com/2004/20041025/kinga.shtml (accessed February 4, 2010).

Chapter Six

p. 122: "hero's journey . . .": Joseph Campbell, *The Hero with a Thousand Faces*, Princeton, NJ: Princeton University Press, 1968.

Chapter Seven

p. 128: For further discussion of King criticism, *see*: works by Michael Collings of Pepperdine University and Tony Magistrale of the University of Vermont.

p. 128: "The popular culture movement . . .": Gary Hoppenstand, ed., *The Journal of Popular Culture*, MI: Michigan State University, https://www.msu.edu/~tjpc/ (accessed on January 29, 2010).

p. 129: For further examples of academic criticism, *see*: Gail E. Burns, "Women, Danger, and Death: The Perversion of the Female Principle in Stephen King's Fiction," *Sexual Politics and Popular Culture*, Bowling Green, OH: Bowling Green State University Press,

1990, 158–172; Mary Findley, "Stephen King's Vintage Ghost-Cars," *Spectral America: Phantoms and the National Imagination*, Madison: University of Wisconsin Popular Press, 2004, 207–220.

p. 129: "*Modern Critical Views* . . .": Harold Bloom, *Stephen King*, rev. ed., New York: Chelsea House, 2007.

p. 130: For additional reference books, guide, and websites, *see*: Stanley Wiater, Christoper Golden, and Hank Wagner, *The Complete Stephen King Universe: A Guide to the Worlds of Stephen King*, New York: Saint Martin's, 2006; Stephen J. Spignesi, *The Complete Stephen King Encyclopedia: A Definitive Guide to the Works of America's Master of Horror*, New York: Contemporary Books, 1993; Bev Vincent, *The Road to the Dark Tower: Exploring Stephen King's Magnum Opus*, New York: NAL, 2004.

p. 130: "tales of the most dastardly . . .": Chelsea Quinn Yarbro, "Cinderella's Revenge: Twists on fairy tales and mythic themes in Stephen King," in *Fear Itself: The Horror Fiction of Stephen King*, eds. Tim Underwood and Chuck Miller, San Francisco: Underwood-Miller, 1982, 45–55.

p. 132: For further discussion of the gothic tale, *see*: Ben P. Indick, "King and the Literary Tradition of Horror and the Supernatural," *Bloom*, 5–16; Tony Magistrale, "Tracing the Gothic Inheritance: *Danse Macabre*," *Bloom*, 59–65; Gary Hoppenstand and Ray B. Browne, eds., *The Gothic World of Stephen King: Landscape of Nightmares*, Bowling Green, OH: Bowling Green State University Press, 1987.

p. 132: "King has described an encounter . . .": Jill Owens, "The Once and Future King," Powell's City of Books, 2006, www.powells.com/authors/stephenking.html (accessed January 29, 2010).

p. 133: "The *New York Times* reported . . .": David D. Kirkpatrick, "A Literary Award for Stephen King," *New York Times*, September

15, 2003, www.nytimes.com/2003/09/15/books/a-literary-award-for-stephen-king.html (accessed February 4, 2010).

p. 134–135: "I salute the National Book Foundation Board…" Stephen King, National Book Awards Acceptance Speech, New York, NY, November 19, 2003, http://www.nationalbook.org/nbaacceptspeech_sking.html (accessed February 4, 2010).

p. 135: "It's not a big deal . . .": Nathaniel Rich, "Interview with Stephen King," *Paris Review*, 178, Fall 2006, www.parisreview.com/viewinterview.php/prmMID/5653 (accessed January 29, 2010).

p. 136: "Fiedler predicted . . .": Bruce Bauman, "The Critic in Winter," *Salon.com*, January 2, 2003, http://dir.salon.com/story/books/int/2003/01/02/fiedler/index.html (accessed January 29, 2010).

p. 136: "Carrie at the prom . . .": Ron Charles, "Art of Darkness," *Washington Post*, October 29, 2006, BW3.

p. 136: "a gray zone…": Ross Douthat, "Stephen King's American Apocalypse," *First Things*, 170, February 1, 2007, www.firstthings.com/article/2007/05/stephen-kings-american-apocalypse-43 (accessed January 29, 2010).

p. 138: "his sheer need to write…" Bruce Handy, "Monster Writer," *Time*, September 12, 1996, http://www.time.com/time/magazine/article/0,9171,985062-2,00.html (accessed January 29, 2010).

p. 138: "Being a brand name is all right . . .": Stephen King, "On Becoming a Brand Name," in *Fear Itself: The Horror Fiction of Stephen King*, eds. Tim Underwood and Chuck Miller, San Francisco: Underwood-Miller, 1982, 42.

p. 138: "I've never denied . . .": Susan Stamberg, "Taking Stephen King Seriously," *Morning Edition*, National Public Radio, November 19, 2003, www.npr.org/templates/story/story.php?storyId=1510901 (accessed February 4, 2010).

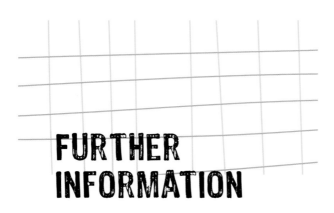

FURTHER INFORMATION

Further Reading

Baughan, Michael Gray. *Stephen King*. New York: Chelsea House, 2009.

Bloom, Harold, ed. *Stephen King*. rev. ed., Modern Critical Views series. New York: Chelsea House, 2007.

Magistrale, Anthony. *Discovering Stephen King's "The Shining."* 2nd ed. San Bernardino, CA: Borgo Press, 2008.

Parish, James Robert. *Stephen King, Author*. New York: Ferguson, 2005.

Rolls, Albert. *Stephen King: A Biography*. Westport, CT: Greenwood, 2009.

Spignesi, Stephen J. *The Essential Stephen King: The Greatest Novels, Short Stories, Movies, and Other Creations of the World's Most Popular Writer*. Franklin Lakes, NJ: New Page, 2001.

Websites

CBS series on Stephen King
www.cbs.com/originals/stephen_kings_n
On this site fans of King's works can see episodes of an original online video series based on his story "N." The series, produced by the CBS network, consists of twenty-five short episodes animated in the style of a graphic novel.

Horror King
www.horrorking.com/
A well-organized collection that includes interviews, brief descriptions of King's books, a filmography, and photos of King and his family; it also includes "Stephen King Rare Works," a list of stories that have not been collected into anthologies.

Lilja's Library: The World of Stephen King
www.liljas-library.com/
A fan site with interviews, news, and information about Stephen King and his work; the site is recommended by King's own website.

New York Times
www.nytimes.com/books/97/03/09/lifetimes/king.html?_r=1
This site contains links to *New York Times* reviews of Stephen King's books and to a thirty-six-minute interview of King's 1994 appearance on the PBS radio program *Fresh Air*.

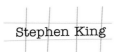

Stephen King's National Book Award Acceptance Speech
www.nationalbook.org/nbaacceptspeech_sking.html
Stephen King's acceptance speech after receiving the National Book Award in 2003.

Stephen King's official website
www.stephenking.com
It includes announcements about new releases of the author's work, a list of his published works, a short biography, an interactive game based on a model of King's business office, an FAQ that answers dozens of the most common questions King receives from his fans, and galleries of personal photos and book covers.

"Umney's Last Case"
http://onlinebooks.library.upenn.edu/webbin/book/lookupname?key=King%2C%20Stephen
"Umney's Last Case," a 1993 short story by King, can be read for free online at this site; the story appears in print in the collection *Nightmares and Dreamscapes*.

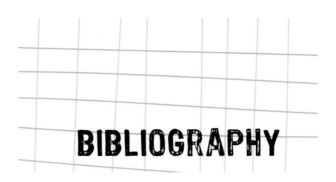

BIBLIOGRAPHY

Beahm, George. *Stephen King: America's Best-Loved Boogey-man*. Kansas City, MO: Andrews McMeel, 1998.

Browne, Ray, and Gary Hoppenstand, eds. *The Gothic World of Stephen King: Landscape of Nightmares*. Bowling Green, OH: Bowling Green State University Popular Press, 1987.

Collings, Michael. *Scaring Us to Death*: *The Impact of Stephen King on Popular Culture*. Rev. ed. San Bernardino, CA: Borgo Press, 2007.

Edmundson, Mark. *Nightmare on Main Street: Angels, Sadomasochism, and the Culture of Gothic*. Cambridge, MA: Harvard University Press, 1997.

King, Stephen. "Why We Crave Horror Movies." *Playboy*, January 1981, 237.

Lant, Kathleen Margaret, and Theresa Thompson, eds. *Imagining the Worst: Stephen King and the Representation of Women*. Westport, CT: Greenwood, 1998.

Leonard, John. "King of High and Low." *New York Review of Books* 49, 2 (February 14, 2002): 32–35.

Magistrale, Tony, ed. *The Dark Descent: Essays Defining Stephen King's Horrorscape*. Westport, CT: Greenwood, 1992.

———. *Discovering Stephen King's "The Shining"*. 2nd ed. San Bernardino, CA: Borgo Press, 2008.

———. *Hollywood's Stephen King*. New York: Palgrave Macmillan, 2003.

———. *Moral Voyages of Stephen King*. 2nd ed. San Bernardino, CA: Borgo Press, 2008.

———. *Stephen King, the Second Decade*: *"Danse Macabre" to "The Dark Half"*. New York: Twayne, 1992.

Miller, Brenda, et al., eds. *Reading Stephen King: Issues of Censorship, Student Choice, and Popular Literature*. Urbana, IL: National Council of Teachers of English, 1997.

Mouhiban, Alec. "Stephen King, Scary Pest." *The American Spectator*, October 31, 2007. http://spectator.org/archives/2007/10/31/stephen-king-scary-pest/ (accessed February 4, 2010).

Reino, Joseph. *Stephen King, the First Decade: From "Carrie" to "Pet Sematary"*. Boston: Twayne, 1988.

Rogak, Lisa. *Haunted Heart: The Life and Times of Stephen King*. New York: Saint Martin's Press, 2008.

Russell, Sharon A. *Revisiting Stephen King: A Critical Companion*. Westport, CT: Greenwood, 2002.

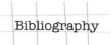

———. *Stephen King: A Critical Companion*. Westport, CT: Greenwood, 1996.

Singer, Mark. "What Are You Afraid Of?" the *New Yorker*, September 7, 1998, 56–61.

Spignesi, Stephen J. *The Lost Work of Stephen King*. Secaucus, NJ: Birch Lane, 1998.

Strengell, Heidi. *Dissecting Stephen King: From the Gothic to Literary Naturalism*. Madison: University of Wisconsin Popular Press, 2005.

Underwood, Tim, and Chuck Miller, eds. *Bare Bones: Conversations with Stephen King*. New York: Warner, 1988.

———. *Fear Itself: The Early Works of Stephen King*. San Francisco: Underwood-Miller, 1993.

———. *Feast of Fear: Conversations with Stephen King*. New York: Carroll and Graf, 1989.

———. *Kingdom of Fear: The World of Stephen King*. New York: New American Library, 1986.

Vincent, Bev. *The Road to "The Dark Tower": Exploring Stephen King's Magnum Opus*. New York: New American Library, 2004.

Wiater, Stanley, Christopher Golden, and Hank Wagner. *The Stephen King Universe: A Guide to the Worlds of the King of Horror*. Los Angeles: Renaissance, 2001.

Winter, Douglas E. *Stephen King: The Art of Darkness*. New York: Signet, 1986.

INDEX

Page numbers in **boldface** are illustrations. A (C) denotes a fictional character.

ABOUT THE AUTHOR

Before becoming a full-time freelance writer, **REBECCA STEFOFF** taught literature classes at Temple University and also at the University of Pennsylvania, where she created and taught that university's first courses in fantasy and science fiction. Her many nonfiction books for young adults include critical biographies of writers: *Herman Melville* (Julian Messner, 1994) and *Jack London: An American Original* (Oxford University Press, 2002). Stefoff explored the territory of horror fiction in *Vampires, Zombies, and Shape-Shifters* (2008), one of five books she wrote for the series Secrets of the Supernatural, published by Marshall Cavendish Benchmark. She has also written on many topics in history and science. Information about Rebecca Stefoff and her books for young people can be found at www.rebeccastefoff.com.